OTHER BOOKS BY SCOTT BYORUM:

The A.M. God
TRIDENT
Dooley Downs

HIEROPHANT

Scott Byorum

Order this book online at www.trafford.com
or email orders@trafford.com

Most Trafford titles are also available at major online book retailers.

Print information available on the last page.

ISBN: 978-1-6987-0258-2 (sc)
ISBN: 978-1-6987-0257-5 (hc)
ISBN: 978-1-6987-0259-9 (e)

Library of Congress Control Number: 2020914143

Trafford rev. 08/14/2020

Trafford PUBLISHING® www.trafford.com
North America & international
toll-free: 1 888 232 4444 (USA & Canada)
fax: 812 355 4082

To Angela…

"Understanding is constrained by questions unasked."
~ SEB

"That's silly."
~ Famous Last Words

"Faith is the assurance of things hoped for; the conviction of things not seen"
~ Some Minister who doesn't know shit, but came up with the perfect definition of Faith; that's not a judgement... I don't know shit either

"It's not the animal itself; it is the air or water that moves the animal. A fish does not swim; it is swum. A bird does not fly; it is flown."
~ Viktor Schauberger

Q: "Why don't snowballs make good golf balls?"
A: "Because they're too cold."
~ RKHKH

CONTENTS

INTRODUCTION

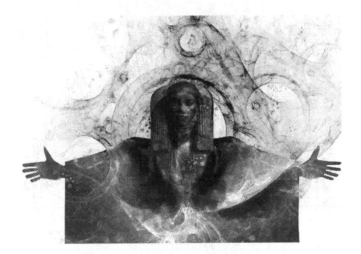

Tarot

N

I'm a fleeting spark in the Ocean's dalliance
By night I'm a Dreamer
By day I'm asleep
I am sometimes a Scorpio
I am always a Fool

I

He is the Magician
The Illusionist of Lies
The blackness of His heart
Is revealed within His eyes
As His soul moves on

II

A pillar of Light
A pillar of Dark
With veins of each shared between
The Ancient Lessons learned in order
From Parent to Child

III

She is the Ruler
She is the Giver
The Empress makes you a Believer
The Seasons will come and go
And She will carry you Home

IV

He is the King
He is the Master
The Emperor rules the World
He is the Fortune
And he is the Pain

V

Between Heaven and Hell
Between Pleasure and Pain
The Hierophant burns
A life with brief name
A time of short reign

VI

You and Me
Locked in embrace
Lost in each other
Our Planets and Signs
The Lovers unite

VII

A Child's toy
The Chariot of God
The Elements churn
And return to the Source
In the palm of an Alien hand

VIII

You are the Strength
You carry through the Ages
I can't do what You do
It's not a burden
It's a gift

IX

The Gate of the Sun
The Hermit within
The Knowledge of the Ages resides
Ancient and forlorn
The Future tries to find

X

Round and round
Our Fortunes to find
The baubles besiege our eyes
Those illusory delights
Those empty treasures

XI

There is weight in forgiveness
There is pain in revenge
There is no taking it back
Only taking it forward
For Justice or worse

XII

The Traitor is a Hanged Man
The Captor is the same
Everyone is right inside their Mind
We borrow from each other
And claim it as our own

XIII

This is the End
Death is the End
The Light between the Towers
Through which everyone must pass
To fertilize a Rose

XIV

The liquids go in
The liquids go out
They transfer from vessel to vessel
Temperance is a Virtue
Temperance is a Sin

XV

Apocalyptic anger
Betrayal and regret
Power is the source of all our lies
Symbols can illuminate
The Devil can control them

XVI

This is the Tower
This is the Fortress
The illusion of safety
The certainty of destruction
Over and over again

XVII

Here comes the Star
Here comes the Light
Here comes the change
Here comes the pain
Here comes your life

XVIII

Whatever you see
Is last in your mind
But changes the World around you
The Moon is a mirror
To share someone's life

XIX

The Sun is here
The Sun is now
The flowers grow
The Red Flag blows
We cherish our lives together

XX

Gabriel blows the Horn
And the Light of God shines upon us
Judgement has come
The Dead will rise
The Living will fall

XXI

The Snake eats its tail
And the World is renewed
The Kingdom of Animals rises and falls
Here comes the Beginning
Here comes the End

HIEROPHANT

A Million Years

And I don't want to see you
For awhile
And I don't want to see you
For awhile
And I don't want to see you
For awhile
And I don't want to see you
Not for a million years

But I am going to miss you
For awhile
But I am going to miss you
For awhile
But I am going to miss you
For awhile
Yeah I am going to miss you
For a million years

But I am going to hate you
For awhile
Yes I am going to hate you
For awhile
Yeah I am going to hate you
For awhile
But I am going to love you
For a million years

A Non-Song

It all goes by so fast
It all goes by so fast
Then it goes by faster
Then it goes by faster

Distressing and depressing
Maddeningly messy
Your heart gets tugged in all directions
Until it aches
Until it breaks
Until it falls apart

When you're young you can't wait
When you're old it's too late
One day comes your fate
And then the mourning

Then dawns the Morning
Of a brand-new day
Of a brand-new day
Each play changes the game
Countless rudders steering the way
Come and stay
Come and stay
Then go away
Then go away

A Song for the Seasons

January embers
Nestle in the hearth
Fueling warmth into our souls
Deep is the Winter
For those kept apart
Smoldering Love's captive coals

The Winter offers
Little reprieve
From the harsh and swirling chill
February sweets
Tucked under sleeve
As a Lover's delight to fulfill

March breathes renew
Into creatures of slumber
The stirring of Motherly natures
Sanguine in Spring
The seeds in their umber
Draw upon the Season's allures

Showers converge
Clean fills the senses
Foliage sprouts verdant and lithe
April's ballet
Through flowery fields
Our spirits encouraged and blithe

May is the slender
Satchel of flowers
Offered to maids in waiting
Suitable tenders
To active desires
Drawn to the pull of the baiting

Lemonade stands
And grasshopper songs
Inspire warm Summer musings
June passes slowly
Active and long
To the whim of everyone's choosing

July soon arrives
Sweat to the brow
As picnics alight on the lawn
Sprinkler rainbows
And firework shows
Carry our courage along

The Dog Days of Summer
Stifle our hearts
We long for the beach and a beer
August vacations
Humid and hot
Alas a new Season draws near

September sends us
Back into schedule
Summer fades slowly away
Rough leather pigskin
The crack of the bat
Warriors resume the Year's play

Autumn leaves
Crackle and fold
Full of fiery brightness
October breezes
Chilly and bold
Our shadows blown steeply behind us

November passes
With giving of thanks
Providing a measure of asking
What does it matter
When passion is frank
And love is not lost in the masking?

Rain and snow
And days of fog
The fleeting of daylight and time
December passes
With festivals bright
And notions of treasures and pine

Age of Rage

Our President is busy
With alternative facts
The News thinks he is crazy
By the way that he acts
Provocative actions
Are beyond all compare
Psychotic notions
Coalesce in despair

Our Nation is in mourning
As Democracy fails
But everything is normal
As it is beyond the pale
They all believe Him
Except for His base
Reality crumbles
Except for His face

His antics get ratings
On that he relies on
Nobody flinches
When somebody dies on

A major disaster
Is all that it takes
No one has answers
With the Rich on the Take
There go your freedoms
Succumbing to fear
It's all about Money
At the expense of the Little Man's tears

Alien Desires

The desire for a liquid diet
The desire to pee outdoors
The rubbing legs
The equilibrium and vertigo problems
The desire for hallucinations
The desire to smoke
Needing less sleep
Dreams that aren't dreams
More vivid actual dreams
Being able to suddenly play somebody's body like music

Being cold when used to always be hot
Can't open my eyes
Massively suppressed appetite
Ability to orgasm dozens of times
Tired often
Mental disconnection

Alien desires

All the Bells on Earth

Maybe in The End
You hear all the Bells on Earth
Toy bells dinging
Church bells singing
Christmas bells chiming
Charity bells pleading
Town bells gonging
Dinner bells calling
Door bells ringing
Wind chimes tinkling
All the Bells on Earth

The last thing you see
Is the shadow of a person in a doorway
It's as simple as that

All the Demons

They can't see me crying through the rain
More than they know
They can't believe
They can't believe that they're wrong

I'm a shadow following your tread
Someone has lied
Manufacture a new start
Initiate a new choice and show love

You cannot hurt me when I'm in the grave
The time is lost
Follow your heart
Follow your voice to your Soul

All these Demons floating through the air
Swallow them whole
You know they're yours
Embrace their mists and move on

All Will Fade

The long lost days
Time passing swiftly
Smiles and laughter become distant echoes
Tears and sorrow embed themselves in the Earth
And then you are dying
And that will be hard
And then you are dying
And you will know your heart
And then you are dying
And the truth will come out
And then you are dying
And what you're about
And you're dying
All has been played
And you're dying
All has been said
You're dying
Time will fade
You're dying
Light goes away
You're dying
All will fade
All will fade

Alone

Take it slow now
Take it slow now
Take it slow now
Criss-cross my heart

And you know now
And you know now
And you know now
All bets are off

Come take my Soul now
Come take my Soul now
Come take my Soul now
Serenade my parts

Free will fulfillment
Free will fulfillment
Free will fulfillment
Or all is for naught

Don't make me grovel
Don't make me grovel
Don't make me grovel
Send me aloft

Begging your employment
Begging your employment
Begging your employment
Negotiating nothing

Heartbeat
Heartbreak
Take the extreme

No fake
Forsake
It's what it seems

But I know the play
Balance the beam
But comes the day
Dreams come to dreams

Alone
Alone
I am alone
Life
Death
Inbetween
I am alone

Am I Today?

How came you upon this land?
Wanderer
Rogue Marine
How came you to distance this?
Callow Fool
Conjurer

My eyes beseech a missive
A shallow pool
A swath of sweat
My lies conceive a Mystic
With ample gold
And frankincense

I wear a mask
Am I today?
Am I today?
I bear a flask
Am I today?
Am I today?
I breach the cask
Am I today?
Am I today?
I toll the task
So come what may
So come what may

Alas I am a God today
With groveling
Caressing hands
Alas I am a following
With blood to sell
And tragedy
So come what may
So come what may
So come what may

Another Day on Earth

Another day on Earth
Full of laughter
High with mirth
People join together
To celebrate their lives
And then they die

I run my trembling hands
Through your thick hair
Over your smooth arms
Down your creamy thighs
And then your lips
And then your lips

Another day on Earth
Living learning
Sowing the soil
People need each other
To fortify their lives
Then they die

I run my trembling hands
Through your thick hair
Over your smooth arms
Down your creamy thighs
And then your breasts
And then your breasts

Another day on Earth
Making money
Thrashing fists
People beat each other
To fornicate their lives
And then they die

I run my trembling hands
Through your thick hair
Over your smooth arms
Down your creamy thighs
And then your lips
And then your lips

Are You Alone Now?

This is where they eat
This is where they sleep
This is where they fornicate
This is where they chop up meat

Ages passing by
Are you alone now?
Are you alone now?
Ages passing by
Are you alone now?
Are you alone now?

This is where they meet
Within the Lonely Castle
Daddy's got the heat
And Mommy's got the hassle

And Daughter is prim and preen
While Brother beats the sheets
The Cat is in the corner
Growling at something small

Ages passing by
Are you alone now?
Are you alone now?
Ages passing by
Are you alone now?
Are you alone now?

Here dawns the hidden score
A gut shot full of fear
The Animals come out to play
And whisper in your ear

This is where the lies evolve
As if it really mattered
This is where the feelings crawl
Blind bound and tattered

Ages passing by
Are you alone now?
Are you alone now?
Ages passing by
Are you alone now?
Are you alone now?

High up in the Tower burns a coal
Nothing ever stays the Game
Even when they call your Name
You're just another cold receding Soul

Ages passing by
Are you alone now?
Are you alone now?
Ages passing by
Are you alone now?
Are you alone now?

Heaven is above
And Hell is below
Below
Below
Below
Heaven is above
And Hell is in tow

Are you alone now?

Atomic

What do I hope to find?
An atomic lust in my mind
An aromatic vapor trapped in plants wrapped in paper

Something is sublime
A moment lost in Time
A general calculation from an unassuming station

Here we go
Here it comes
Time to enjoy frenzy
Time to employ fun

Orange and red the blossom blooms
Paint peels back the hidden room
Soon comes back the scene to loom
Night becomes Noon

What do I hope to find?
An atomic lust in my mind
In aromatic ashes lost in dust wrapped in time

Space music
Heard from long ago
An unassuming world trapped in beauty wrapped in snow

At the Door

Daddy is at the door
I have no patience
Because I crave spaceships

Mommy is at the door
I'll ease your crying
If you stop lying

Brother is at the door
I punch you around
Because you're a quaint little Clown

Beauty is at the door
I kinda like you
But I don't really like you

Girlfriend is at the door
I don't want your semen
Because I like women

Lover is at the door
For decades
Now I don't love you
Because I thought I could change you
You didn't like my Mother
Neither did I
You were never there for me
Even though you were
So I re-wrote History
So it is all your fault

No one is at my door
No one befriends
No one sends

Reaper is at my door
Not a good contact
Not a fair contract

God is at my door
Nothing to say
Please go away

Demon is at my door
Is everybody in?
The show is about to begin

Devil is at my door
Pleased to meet you
Hope you guess my name

Nothing is at my door
But the Wind
Always the Wind

Backhand

You screwed up your life Son
You screwed up your life
You screwed up your life Son
You screwed up your life

I told you once or twice Son
I told you once or twice
And you screwed up your life Son
You screwed up your life

You screwed up my life Dad
You screwed up my life
I told you once or twice Dad
I told you once or twice

The backhand is invisible
The backhand is each word
The backhand indivisible
From back of hand
From Word of Man

Backhand
Backhand
Every day
Every way
Backhand
Backhand
Backhand
Backhand

Backhand

Banshee

The Moaning Woman walks this way
Why O Why
Why O Why
The Moaning Woman walks this way
Why O Why
Why O Why

Moaning about the Winter
Moaning about the cold
Why O Why
Why O Why
Moaning about lonely
Moaning about Home
Why O Why
Why O Why

Have you seen her walk this street?
Have you seen her cry?
Have you felt the Winter's chill?
And do you know now why?

The Moaning Woman walks this way
Why O Why
Why O Why
The Moaning Woman walks this way
Why O Why

Beginning's End

Everything that's created
Comes to an end
Begin again
Begin again

Everything that's created
Comes to an end
Begin again
Begin again

Shiva engages in The Dance
Shiva makes the Earth sing
Wipe the slate clean
Wipe the slate clean

Shiva engages in The Dance
Shiva makes the Earth sing
Wipe the slate clean
Wipe the slate clean

Breaking stones
Now we dance
Clashing swords
Now we dance
Smashing atoms
Now we dance
Wipe the slate clean
Wipe the slate clean
Begin again
Begin again

Be Free

All your life is on Throne
All you try is all you own
Here comes now the fate of ease
When all your will is on your knees
Be free

Heaven is for those who wait
Not for those who hesitate
You'll never see the time you waste
You won't recall the taste you ate
Be free

Take the time to know your fate
Taste the food upon your plate
Fire is not your only friend
Leaves will blow and limbs will bend
Be free

I can see you in the past
I can't recall though when the last
Touch your mind and you will see
The nuances of you and me
Be free

Black Cat

The Cat's body drips over the ledge
Like black crude oil in slow motion
She plops down onto the plush carpet
And slinks Her way to my whereabouts
Pouncing on my lap
[needles and pins]
She curls up into the crux of my leg
Like a thick breathing furry blanket
Purring ensues
As She looks into my eyes lazily
She nibbles softly at my fingers
And glides Her whiskers along my hands
Compelling
So I honor Her request
And pet Her soft hair
Over and over
Until She quietly falls asleep
And I am stuck

Broken Things

Things I've had have come and gone
Have come and gone
Have come and gone
Things I've had have come and gone
From my eye to my mind
From my mind to my eye

Things I have are flown and gone
Have are flown and gone
Have are flown and gone
Things I have are flown and gone
From my eye to my mind
From my mind to my eye

Have you seen that lovely gown?
Floating on the wind
Floating on the wind
That lovely gown has flown and gone
From my life to my mind
From my life to my eye

Burn the Witch

Whoa to the World
I am here to stay
I am a Harbinger
Entropy ensues

Burn the Witch

They hunt them on the Prayer Lines
So obvious
So obtuse
Few are looking
I have a plan

Burn the Witch

Here I am again
In a wonderous way
I bring awareness
As I breeze away

Burn the Witch

Button Down Doll

She's in love
With her Button Down Doll
With her Button Down Doll
She's in love
She's in love

She picks her nose
With her Button Down Doll
With her Button Down Doll
She picks her nose
She picks her nose

She sucks her thumb
With her Button Down Doll
With her Button Down Doll
She sucks her thumb
She sucks her thumb

She pulls her hair
With her Button Down Doll
With her Button Down Doll
She pulls her hair
She pulls her hair

She slaps her face
With her Button Down Doll
With her Button Down Doll
She slaps her face
She slaps her face

She breathes fast
With her Button Down Doll
With her Button Down Doll
She breathes fast
She breathes fast

She makes love
With her Button Down Doll
With her Button Down Doll
She makes love
She makes love

She lays quiet
With her Button Down Doll
With her Button Down Doll
She lays quiet
She lays quiet

Childhood

Childhood is a special place
Childhood is an open face
It occupies a grace
Inside our hearts
Though quite menial and commonplace
Childhood is a maze

Childhood is a memory
Childhood is a fantasy
Moments of glorious revelry
A time of tears
And wounded knee
A long and aching brevity

Childhood is a happiness
Childhood is a horror
It tends to build you up inside
But boredom is its borders
Childhood is empty magic thoughts
It will show you where to hide
So you can hide

Close to Me

My head starts drumming
When you walk a little close to me
My heart starts humming
When you walk a little close to me
It starts humming
It starts humming

A little closer to me
A little closer to me
It starts humming
It starts drumming

Teetering on a wire
I stoked a fire
I stoked a fire

I took your will
I stole your power
I plucked you like a flower

You call me crazy
I call it realize
Now you realize
Now you realize
Now you realize
Now you realize
Now you realize
Now you realize

Cold Part of Warmth

Paper news
And paper lies
And plastic figurines

Moonless views
And starry nights
And endless magazines

You're the cold part of warmth
You're the depth in the seams
You're the cold part of warmth
You're the depth in the seams

I had you once
I had you twice
I've satisfied your dreams

I've gone away
Nowhere to stay
The cracks lie inbetween

You're the cold part of warmth
You're the depth in the seams
You're the cold part of warmth
You're the depth in the seams

Commence the Heartache

He was scanning the horizon
He was bludgeoned by thought
He was heavy with the music
Of the feelings he bought

She was peering past the Pyramid
She was punished by pride
She was picking through the music
Avoiding her lies

Who collects the little sleights?
Who houses the nuts?

Now convince
Convince the Heartache
Now convince
Convince the Heartache
Now convince
Convince the Heartache
Now you don't have nothing now

An Empath goes down
To the River by the Bay
Memories come around
And they play where they may

Who collects the little sleights?
Who comforts the nuts?

Now commence
Commence the Heartache
Now commence
Commence the Heartache
Now commence
Commence the Heartache
Now you don't have nothing now

Coward

You're going to splay your demonstrations
You're gonna stomp your feet and shout
In the end your machinations
Disappear inside your mouth

You don't have to turn around to see me
I won't be the photo on your wall
You can only have so much
Remembering from our last touch
And I bet you will ever fail to notice

You can smell the masturbation
Slathering your hands
There's no need to look abused
There's no way to make amends

You don't have to listen up to hear me
I won't be the voice inside your head
The pages that record these words
Are all of me you've ever heard
And I bet you won't ever fail to notice

You've got a narrow scope of viewing
There're other colors in the pack
You need to extract another crayon
You need to draw another map

You keep on living in your lonely private nightmare
Did anybody ever show you how to change?
The little power that it set in you
Has come undone and you're the Fool
And you keep dancing in the circle of a Coward

You're gonna reach your destination
With every road you take
Every threshold bears the answer
Every keyhole twists your fate

Crows and Chimes

Crows and chimes
Crows and chimes
What's yours is yours
And what's mine is mine
Your empty cards
Sung with vacant lies
And hung with swift goodbyes

Much of what is told is told with perfect perspective
Perfect perspective
Perfect perspective
Much of what is lost is lost with perfect perspective
Perfect perspective
Perfect perspective

And still we tell
And still we judge
And still we lose
And we send cards

Chimes and crows
Chimes and crows
What's mine is yours
And what's yours is mine
Your beautiful thoughts
And your serpentine minds
Are packed with dull goodbyes

Crows Nesting On Power Lines

The mask behind the mirror
The figure in the doorway
The light behind the frame
He knows my name
It's all the same

And there they are
Crows nesting on power lines
Biding their time

The dust upon the antique clock
The picture in the doorway
The doilies and the chair that rocks
Watch it rock
Just like a clock

And there they were
Pins nesting on battle plans
Biding their time

Days of Mirrored Pasts

Living without you and how I was
Living without you and how I want
Now I'm a child again

I have to recognize
When I come across as blithe
In days of mirrored pasts

I could miss her by seconds
I could miss her by hours
I could see her in the twilight
I could see her through the showers

And they settled on their banal lives
And reveled in the blithe
In days of mirrored pasts

I've seen the lights and heard the noises
Incongruently cavorting
Through days of mirrored pasts

Destination

We're all headed to the same place same place
We're all headed to the same place

We all think that we are right inside our head

How lives change
And we don't
There's a million miles to freedom
There's the everyday of pain
What are you running from?
Where are you going to?
Feel the drain

Part of me wants to say you are right
But ultimately you are wrong
We all are
About everything
So just let go
Just learn to let go
And sing the song of a Swan

I have to deal with this deal with this deal with this
You have to deal with this

The whole World has to deal with this

Devil May Care

Hold that sight
Devil may care
Devil may fight
But He don't fight fair

But you know when you're winning right?

And that night will come to you
Staring down a long gun steel barrel
And that flight will come to you
It will chill you to the marrow

Hold that sight
Devil may care
Devil may fight
But He don't fight fair

But you know when you're winning right?

And that plight will befall you
As you scamper through the shadows
No might will console you
As you surrender what was borrowed

Hold that sight
Devil may care
Devil may fight
But He don't fight fair

But you know when you're winning right?

Someone there deplores you
As you navigate the narrative
But I must then implore you
To seek the sole imperative

Hold that sight
Devil may care
Devil may fight
But He don't fight fair

But you know when you're winning right?

Dirty Pictures

Traveling around beach time
I begin to feel that she wants more
Sadness has an agenda
And it's often love that pays dearly

Written words become the illusion
Time slips away from emotion
Compromise belies dead issues
Limited we possess in content

Heaven knows I'm insecure
Supermen reside in comics
And Heaven knows you're unaware
Dirty pictures bleeding in the limelight

Heaven knows I'm obsolete
Thought at first it's going to be my time
And Heaven knows you're incomplete
Dirty pictures swinging from the clothesline

You don't have to say that you're worried
You don't have to say anything at all
You don't have to pretend you're hurried right now

I don't want to savor glory
I just want to live my own story
I don't want to be the reason you lie

Dirty pictures besiege our eyes

Disaffected Youth

There's no shoulder
There's no sound
There's just gibbering little ping pongs around
Wrestling on the ground
Yeah
Those young boys rabble rousing
Until a one-eyed coyote pops up
And bites their necks
And their heads all hang like flop
Like tops to come off
And we tied them up
And hunted them varmints by all means possible
Blasting them into buckets
One Bubba cutting his friend with a blow torch
Tearing him new skin
And we were having our cigarettes and drinking gin
Boys gonna leave Momma alone
Take it outside and do as you're told
Boy you'll be going down a terrible Goddamned path
I'll bust you with a hammer
Or pop you with a .45
Have them come around with their contracts
Around 10 or 11:30 with their best new contacts
Put a Buffalo on my head and throw me in the Slammer
I'm talking to the Man and hearing nine booms
Nine white booms
And he asks about nine Moons
And everything capers not to love me
Water going up and down and all about
And we don't even know what ten million is
And you're making me go over to His voice
So I'm going over to His voice
But then you tell me it's His voice
As long as I don't shit my pants before I die
That's the way it's always been

And I don't want to die
So I'm not trying to die
But there is this guy over here
That just blasted the heads out of his wife and kids
And nobody even talked about it
And the sound you would hear you wouldn't believe
And how did I end up with everyone else in the room?
Just standing around working on presentation?
Everyone telling themselves it's not so bad
When it really is

How is he doing?
He couldn't be better
He couldn't be better
He couldn't be better
Look at him he's dying
He couldn't be better
Doesn't anybody take responsibility for the lives of young men anymore?
I don't know how
When nothing tastes like this

Dominance

You know I'm such a deep roller
I aught to put you in a baby stroller
You're calling
You're calling out

Now you know my name
Now you feel my pain
I'm gonna make you mine
You'll get it
You'll respect

Your mouth is such a pretty socket
Bobbing up and down a swollen rocket
You're crying
You're crying now

Now you know my name
Now you feel my pain
I'm gonna make you mine
You'll get it
You'll respect

I'm not giving you a straight face
My teeth are gritted in a frozen place
I'm laughing
I'm laughing now

Now you know my name
Now you feel my pain
I'm gonna make you mine
You'll get it
You'll respect

Down Done Gone Dark Time

Down
Swallowed by the mist of years
Borne upon a tide of fears
Brought on by a flood of tears

Done
Feigning it was all a spell
Afraid that you will go to Hell
The waste of it was just as well

Gone
Seems like someone knew your name
Seems like part of some Big Game
Seems like seems like all the same

Dark
Nothing new inside your brain
Before you knew of nothing sane
Time becomes an endless frame

Time
No longer part of History
No longer any mystery
No longer any mist of me

Elemental

There are things in this World
Taken for granted
Like fire
Like earth
Like water and air
But not your hair

Fire sounds like water sometimes
Water sounds like air
Do you notice these things?
I wonder

Things that people cared about
Lost in a function of time and feeling
Things integral
Now trivial
Marginalized

All of this moves
Like a heartbeat
Like breathing

Elemental

We will rub the crust from our eyes
A thousand years of motes clogging up clarity
Coagulating our perceptions
Congealing our spirit
It's too late to forget what you already know

Elemental

Empty Nest

Of branches bare
Of leaves have fallen
No tear shed I
Save when Mother is calling

Not in sorrow
To heed her comfort
But for toils past
That paved my path
And filled my heart with fondness

Energy

This energy I feel
So natural with you
I always feel you in me
And near me
Consuming me
Our kisses are like we are reading each other's minds
Anticipating and relishing madly
Rhythm and precision
Our bodies are speaking and responding
With the ease of each other
Our thoughts parallel gorgeously
Your soft skin
That sweet taste of sweat
And whispery perfume
My hands grope
Your luscious curves
I crave you constantly
I want to gingerly ravage your body
I want to make love to you
I love you
Talking
Laughing
Expressing
Touching
I cannot get enough
Every little taste I get of you
Leaves me parched for more

Extreme

You are extreme
It is all or nothing with you
Because you are extreme it makes you an extremist
That makes you intolerant and unreasonable
Being unreasonable makes you irrational
Which means you cannot be objective
It means you do not think clearly
You select facts that only support your own conclusions
And ignore those that refute them
You are extreme
You are dangerous

Faith

What happens to the person who asks?
What happens to the person who doesn't?

Why are we here?
Why can't we stay?
We live and die alone
We waste our time away

Can you cry me a riddle of tears that explains your heart?

Why do we laugh and cry?
Why were we given this pain and joy?
You can do anything
But you cannot do no thing

And what we do best is lie
To ourselves and others
But mostly to ourselves
And to God

What do you want?
What do you do?
Who do you love?
Who loves you?

How many times can I say that I love you?
How many times can I not say it?

Why do we forget things we should remember?
Why do we remember things we should forget?

Why do we so desperately hold onto hate?
And so casually let go of love?

It's not that others cannot forgive you
It's that you can't forgive you
You don't deserve you
Give yourself up
Or give yourself in

I may never meet you
And I may never greet you
And I may never return
And I may never go back

Love is all things
And love is no thing
And I want to go there

Follow me
There's a doorway ahead
Step through

Falling Down

Can't you see can't you see
Can't you see can't you see
There are two in this corner
Can't you see

Saving me saving me
Saving me saving me
It's a lot more than water
Saving me

We're all headed to the same place same place
We're all headed to the same place

Let me be let me be
Let me be let me be
When the World's gone shattered
Let me be

Falling down falling down
Falling down falling down
It's just me on the inside
Falling down

Father

I'm not a Father
So I don't know quite what you've gone through with me
I know I haven't always been
A good Son
And I know at times
You've been impatient
And hard
And I know you've always done the best you could
With the life
And experience
You've been given

That's good enough for me

Know that I love you
No matter what
I try to do the best
With what you've given
And taught me
I don't always succeed
But I'm happy when you forgive me
And I'm happy that you still support my efforts
To get through this mess that is life
And find some measure
Of fulfillment

That's good enough for me

I don't know what will be
But you will always be my Father
And I will always love you
If I could take back all the times
I've hurt you

Or caused you worry
I would
But it is what it is
And we are all flawed
To the core
But we can always do more

That's good enough for me

I hope all of your days are good
Even if they can't all be
But some of them can
And those are the days worth remembering

That's good enough for me

Feeling Every Minute

I always knew it was worth the risk
But now that risk is real
I always knew it was worth the fight
But now that fight is feel
Afraid to change
Afraid of fright
Afraid to rearrange
Afraid of sight
Afraid that I might not survive
In mind or body
To become something strange
Afraid to pay the cost
The cost is lost
Within my body and my brain
Why can't I remain the same?

Lost words
I can feel every minute
Each one longer than the one before
But then time sucks in around me
The future is born
And that is where you find me
Within my sullen scorn
And that is where you find me
Not with ties of bondage
But with lust and love and time
Unrealized
With pity and remorse
Feeling every minute
Of change
Of course

Fighting for Your Life

The loneliness of being alone
The solitude of loneliness
I am in this shell
Fighting for my life
I cower in the corner
I hide amongst my things
All my pleasant pretty things
But I am not a thing
I am beyond things
I am and I will be
Because I am fighting for my life
Death will surely come
Nothing will stop that fate
The end of me
My absence from things
But not now
Not today
I will fight
I will fight for my life
And I will rail against fear
I will strip away my arrogance
Those things that only serve themselves
And when I perish
When I fade and drift away
When the dust of myself folds in and disperses
The thing
The shell that is me
Returns to the soup of spirit and time
I will rest
I will rest with the unknown
Blessed
That I have fought for life
For the temporal
For the gift
The gift that is life

Find Me

Hindsight 20/20
That's where you lord over them
I made the right choices
You were wrong
I was right
You lose
I win
What an empty victory
What a sorrowful defeat

Find me
Find me

Whatever I say
In the deepest
    Darkest
    Depths
Of my desperation
Of my depression
I will be true to you
I will follow grace

Find me
Find me

Frail Predators

Single Mothers are prowling for Fathers
We can be that frail
We can be that frail
Single Fathers are lusting for Daughters
We can be that frail
We can be that frail
That Whore is laced with sin
And the tainted scent of Bad Men
We can be that frail
But now that we are drunk
Scuttled by that liquid skunk
Drowned in droll dollops of funk
Does it really matter
That we are here at all?
We can be that frail

Free Fall

Down the hall
The actions of my feet will take me down the hall
The carrier of my will has now set forth the course
I softly pad my way past all the shuttered doors
But please make no mistake
No one must awake
The gentry of The Giant sleeping on the wall

I recall
The Neurons in my mind have caused me to recall
The blindness in the light has gilded to my sight
And now I have no way of telling what is right
But please make no mistake
The emptiness it makes
Leaves nothing but the feeling of free fall

Bubbles fall
The water cascades to a drain where bubbles fall
And now he puts the pain into that open drain
Where no one ever can discover him again
But please make no mistake
Shivering and shakes
Tend to go unnoticed when there's nothing wrong at all

Ghost Train

You never ask me how my day was
I hold out hoping
But I just won't hold my breath

You're always blabbing about your boyfriends
My heart is breaking
And it just won't heal tonight

You're coming at me like a Ghost Train
You're passing through me like pain

Your pouty lips are like poison
My arms empty
And they just won't fill tonight

Your curvy hips are in motion
You're stepping through me now
And you're stepping out the door

You're coming at me like a Ghost Train
You're passing through me like pain

You're in and in it like passion
I kick myself
For doing nothing positive

You're on and on it like fashion
I'd kill myself
But it would just be negative

You're coming at me like a Ghost Train
You're passing through me like pain

Glory to the King

We drunk our hearts out for you
We smote our bodies on this Earth for you
For this brief brief time
We have all just begun
And suddenly it all unravels
Over and over
As we bang our heads against God's breast
How did it come to this?
How did we get this old?
How did Time steal our face?
Our bodies?
Our souls?
Each thrust of the shovel into the Earth
The first is the worst
And then we are just making a bed
A nest for eternal rest
How do we do this to ourselves?
How do we go on knowing…
Goodbye
Goodbye
Goodbye

God Bless America

God bless America
And we are still here
God bless America
We are what we fear
God bless America
All pain and good cheer

It's a Grande Olde Gun
It's some fast shooting fun
They've got terror in their eyes
They get terror on the run
The sirens will sound
When the shooting's finally done
And we will know we have one

God bless America
And we are still here
God bless America
We are what we fear
God bless America
All pain and good cheer

Growing Down

Far from being free
Walking homeward
And you beat your little paws upon the drum

Crawling and walking and skipping and running

Mount your steel horse
Driving nowhere
And you're working at a desk and having fun

Crawling and walking and skipping and running

Shattering beliefs
Hair growing white
There's a young pup growing up to be your boss

Crawling and walking and skipping and running

Years floating by
Humming lonely
And you don't know what is next or what's to come

Crawling and walking and skipping and running

Happy Pictures

Can there be a truth that's been taught
That cannot be borrowed or sold or bought?
All those orchestrated scores
You want to reign upon your familiars

There are stories in that magic
Strange and uncertain
Unknowing to an eager eye
But upon this how we do rely

You are going to weep
Long and hard
And you are going to curl
Within your slow cocoon
But the end always comes to stow
And nobody can take it

You only need to be sad at your truth
Sad at the World
And sad at your direction
You only need to be sad at your thoughts
Sad at your deeds
And sad at your affections
What is lost?
What is gained?
What is swallowed in time?
Your fabled stories?
Your music box?
Your Mommy's Teddy bear?
More like your hopes and dreams and prayers
And those are fears
And that is the sad return

Happy pictures in an album
Happy pictures on a hard drive
Happy pictures on the clouds
In a magazine
On the treacherous Web
Happy pictures
They make you happy
They make you sad

Hard Case

White light and red blur
The gut is bare and empty
Now it's getting worse

Flash point and live nerve
The signs are floating out there
Bending 'round the curve

Who's rolling with the hard wood?
He's burning up the rubber
So he's understood

Who's standing in the hard rain?
He's gonna make you suffer
Gonna give you pain

Who's pulling on the red wine?
He's smashing down his Ego
Until it gives him Time

Who's dragging on the red flame?
He's breathing fire madness
As he lays his blame

Who's painting down a dark night?
It's all that's left of nothing
And now there's nothing nice

And now it's black
As a starless night

Holocene Drip

And so we are here
Perched upon this pile of Humanity
Humanity
A misnomer
An oxymoron
Life is worthless
That we make out in words as worthwhile
We prove it everyday
War is our way
Butchery is okay
And the Master of Apes holds sway
So we carry on today

So why do I feel guilt?
Why do I feel the pang of conscience?

We are buoyed upon the waters
Of the Holocene Drip
We consume the Nile Perch
And paint the poisons on our lips
Holocene Drip
Holocene Drip
We press it to our lips

House of You

Saturday slumber
Evenings of wine
House of you
House of you

Sunday musings
Saturnine
House of you
House of you

Long weeks
Lost and away
House of you
House of you

Warm cheeks
Tickle and play
House of you
House of you

I've lost the candor to entertain fear
Our love lies here
House of yoo

Hurricane

All the people run
All the people run around
All the people walk
All the people walk and talk

The hurricane inside your mind
The hurricane inside your life
The hurricane inside your tribe
This is where it takes you

Busy little bodies
Doing meaningless things
Filling up their cups
Emptying their minds of all

The hurricane inside your mind
The hurricane inside your life
The hurricane inside your tribe
This is where it takes you

I Am

I am
I am your fate
I am your death and I am your mate

I am
I am your fire
I am your hate and I am desire

I am
I am your want
I am your toil and I am your hunt

I am
I am your while
I am your cunning and cold defile

I am
I am your love
I am escape and nothing above

I am
I am your bode
I am your back and I am your load

I am
I am your judge
I am your justice emerging from mud

I am
I am the way
I am the future of past that you pray

I am
I am no thing

I Get Blind

Light
Light hurts my eyes
I can get blind

Eagles dance in the distant air
Or are they crows?
Clouds of sparrows?
Robins?
I don't know

Have you ever felt two weeks from everywhere?
Two weeks from nowhere?
It takes a shovel and some grit
To get past the painful parts

You are so imperfect
That you are perfect
Unimaginable life all around me
Clouds and swirls
Bounce and twirls
And these flawed eyes

Abandoned souls
And light
Light hurts my eyes
I can get blind

Idle Wastes

Time is a love you can feel in my heart
But it's a love that is fleeting
And it always wants to dissipate away

Sun is a way you can see in my heart
But Sun isn't easy
And it's always going to sear your pretty eyes

Fun is a way to achieve what you start
But fun can be boring
If you really don't have anything to say

Maybe you've been thinking hard
Walking down the boulevard
Waiting for that song to start
Watching people moving cars

Maybe you've been thinking hard
Walking down the boulevard
Pining with a broken heart
Chasing shadows in the dark

Maybe you've been thinking hard
Walking down the boulevard
Passing through the doors of bars
Plucking at an old guitar
And nourishing your idle wastes

I Feel the Smell of Life

I feel the smell of perspiration, work, and toil
I feel the smell of earth, grass, and flowers
I feel the smell of touching, kissing, and lovemaking
I feel the smell of warm and wise connection
I feel the smell of learning about and knowing someone else
I feel the smell of the majesty and brilliance of living things
I feel the smell of time passing constantly and forever
I feel the smell of fresh blossoms and vibrant Springs
I feel the smell of hot pavement and long Summer days
I feel the smell of scattering leaves and lonely Fall evenings
I feel the smell of cool breezes and chilly Winters
I feel the smell of loss and grievance
I feel the smell of distant memories that alter my current perceptions
I feel the smell of waste and uselessness
I feel the smell of hatred, ignorance, and intolerance and the shame that washes over my senses
I feel the smell of poverty, hunger, suffering, and Death that blazes upon my television screen and newspaper headlines
I feel the smell of the horror of war and the intractable decision to wage it
I feel the smell of soft, warm paws in my hands and the unconditional love that sparkles in those wide, wondering eyes

I'm Not Missing Anything

Things will wake you up
Things will make you sleep
Things will make you choke
Things will make you weep
Things will instill power
Things will blossom pain
Things will make you glower
Things will bring you shame

I'm not missing anything

Things will make you choose
Things will make you slip
Things will make you lose
Things will cause a flip
Things will cause a crave
Things bring on a cruise
Things manifest a rave
Here arrives the booze

I'm not missing anything

Things will make you look down at the sidewalk when you stroll
Things will make you lose the smile that everyone used to love
The World closes in around you
Time will pass you by
All of this will make you
You

I'm not missing anything

Indigo Street

"I never got over the notion
That I was invincible
And not wanting to be"

I got something going way up yonder
On Indigo Street
Those downtown uptight girls got nothing
Nothing I need

Got a few more drinks now going on here
On Indigo Street
The bartenders all say they belong there
Filling my seat

Hey Jay
We're strolling down
To Indigo Street

Got a sweet fine girl that I want to see
On Indigo Street
Too much fog and fuss for me
Stoking what I need

Can you breathe the air?
Were you ever there?
On Indigo Street
Can you breathe the air?
Were you ever there?
On Indigo Street

Hey Jay
We're trolling down
On Indigo Street

Still not stealing for my bread
On Indigo Street
Still not dreaming of my dread
Still not taking chance
Still afraid to dance
On Indigo Street
Still not selling souls
Gold bowls overflow
But not while Jay and me
Muse the wild and free
As much as you to me
On Indigo Street
On Indigo Street

Hey Jay
We fake amends
Afraid to face the bitter end
On Indigo Street

Hey Jay
We face the day
And each one makes it pass away
On Indigo Street

On Indigo Street

Intangible

My comfort level falls in the Hall of the King
Here we are talking about the same old things
Maybe that appeases the average folk
Not speaking your heart until the other has spoke
What of yourself do you wish to impart to me?
The treasure of your life long exploits?
Is that what you think about me?
My rightful inheritance lies imprisoned behind your ribcage
Encased within your cranium
It is the miles your eyes have traveled
The music your ears have indulged
It dwells in the creases and the folds of your face
Bourne upon the length of every line that mars your palms
What do you think of me and my accomplishments?
Where is the wine that liberates our tongues to speak the truth?
Does the King have pride to bear upon his chest?
Or is he awash in the pain, guilt, and fear of life?
Time is fleeting and loss is certain
The court you hold is changing
And I may only know of myself from that which you don't speak of
That is the true tragedy of the impermanent and the intangible
That which we imagine to fill in the gaps

In the Fathoms of Zeal

Feed your mind into an animal's meal
This is what it feels like
In the fathoms of zeal
Claw your heart with the love that you steal
This is what it feels like
In the fathoms of zeal
Peel your lips back into a horrible squeal
This is what it feels like
In the fathoms of zeal

Running out of all your precious Seasons
Stepping into someone else's reason
Running out of all your precious Seasons
Stepping into someone else's reason

Grabbing the Scroll and breaking its Seal
This is what it feels like
In the fathoms of zeal
Greeting the Preacher with a powerful kneel
This is what it feels like
In the fathoms of zeal
Taking advantage of another in deal
This is what it feels like
In the fathoms of zeal

In Your Hands

Life and Death in your hands
Life and Death in your hands

Watcha gonna do
With your hands?
Watcha gonna do
With your hands?

Life and Death in your hands
Life and Death in your hands

It's all in your mind
And in your hands
It's all in your mind
And in your hands

Life and Death in your hands
Life and Death in your hands

Watcha gonna do
With your hands?
With your hands?
With your hands?

Invisible

When you hit the Season
Believing things you don't believe in
Then you will know there is no reason to the reason

Their sounds will cover my sounds
Their voices will cover my voice
Their smells will cover my smells
Their tastes will cover my tastes
Their sights will cover my sight
Their feelings will cover my feelings
Their thoughts will cover my thoughts
Their actions will cover my actions
Their wishes will cover my wishes
Their projections will cover me
They will cover me

I am invisible

When you hit the Season
Believing things you don't believe in
Then you will know there is no reason to the reason

Last Man Passing

There are places
Never seen
That go on
There are faces
Never known
That go on

There is my life
Never seen
Never known
That moves on

Like Sunday
Like rain
Like moments
Like pain
Like time messing with my mind
Like I'm messing with your kindness

Hang them high
The Hangman's high
We're gonna light the bonfires tonight
We're gonna explore our vanities
We're going to town
Gonna set it alight
We're going to Manhattan
Buy a dozen cause it's cheaper

Love wrecked
I'm wrecked
You're wrecked
Life is wrecked

I'm a Westerner
A ghost in Real Life
Where were the Good Times
I was promised as a child?
They are layers of cake
Colorful and spoiled
You reach your vertical limit
And then you are falling down

Her lips are molten rouge
And I am the Outlander
Maybe she's the Meddler
Maybe I am the Anomaly

At Daylight's end
There's a righteous kill in Freetown
There is momentum in the masses
This is Christmas

I am a Traitor
I am a Dead Man Walking
I am a Dark Horse
Bye bye Love
I am Risen
I am Joy
I am One True Thing
I am a Neutron Star

Now you see me
Now you don't
Now you want me
Now you won't
This is my Secret Life
As Bees around me die
I have heard the cries from Syria
And I've wept at the response

Where is my Sister?
For I miss her
But she never really was
Because nobody kissed her
And 28 days later
I have 127 hours to live
It's either Fate or Choice
But in the End it's lights out

I am the King of Suicides
I am the Master
Of want and waste and want again
Time passes faster
I am The Last Man Standing
I am The Last Man Passing
I am a Dead President
As the money burns the world

There are places
Never seen
That go on
There are faces
Never known
That go on

There is my life
Never seen
Never known

Laugh

Laugh
Laugh at my silliness
Laugh at the only being who thinks God doesn't love him
Laugh at me
Laugh at my lack of faith
Laugh out loud at the lack of my knowledge
Laugh at my arrogance and fear
Laugh at the nature of things
Laugh at the fabric that bounces and binds us
Laugh at time and space and motion
Laugh at the star that spins and burns and travels
Laugh at the exploding universe around you
Laugh at your own stupid and simple desires
Laugh at your wasteful beliefs and transgressions
Laugh at power and control and the illusion they bear
Laugh at what should and should not be
Laugh at what is past and forgotten
Or not
But at least laugh
Laugh at me

Liberation

If I can make it through the Winter
To breathe the morning fumes of Spring
Then I'll have made it
Then I'll have played it

Past the cold clutch of callousness
To the bold branching of Spring
Then I'll be alright
Then I'll breathe the Light

When my world is white
When my world is wide
When my world is why
I live again
I live again
I live again

If I can make it through this dinner
Sunday's searing stare of eyes
Brave the whys
Brave the lies
Brave those eyes
I live again

Lies

You are going to convince yourself of lies
And you are going to convince yourself
That you are the victim
And all of that is true
You are the liar
And you are the victim of your lies

I was once young
And I knew everything
Now I am old
And I know next to nothing
But I do know lies

You are going to convince yourself of lies
And you are going to convince yourself
That you are the victim
And all of that is true
You are the liar
And you are the victim of your lies

Love

And suddenly it's calm
The air
Shrouding us like a growing silence
Moments from a storm
She spoke to me in standard rhythms
Though I'm no normal man
I answered back with self-involvement
And with pen thrust into hand
Love can wrench the heart to pieces
With such passion and such flare
But love can survive the dismal difference
Between fundamental cares
You and I have felt so close
To which nothing can compare
Each time we join
I join with you
But am I the one who's there?
They can offer you security
And fun and laughs and Sun
I offer you the Moon above us
Cold and distant as it may be
But even still
Together
We are One

Love & Death

Singing in the air
Flipping like some bird I can't describe
Flipping like my insides
It goes up
Up
Up
And it comes down
Down
Down

Something that has value
Something in the space between us
Which really isn't there
Just something like a sparkle
To calm our need for fear

Something that gets lost
Something that tumbles and twirls
It rolls its way into the depths
This sewer we call time
A misnomer for something so fine

It's something so simple
So simple that we wrack our brains about it
The flipping of a coin
Light
Light
Light
Dark
Dark
Dark

Love & Death

Little Kid Lost

Dear troubled Son
Life is empty
Life is cold
Throw out your shadow
Cast it out bold
Here come your problems
Here comes the pain
Wherever you journey
Your name is the same
Recognize
You are exactly where you want to be

I come home
It's where I want to be
But I guess I'm already there
I come home
I open up my eyes
And somehow I know that I'm aware
Something offers me just another
Day to realize who I am
Sun has arisen
Another decision
I'm gonna bring out something to bear

I am the gloom in the corner
I am the warned and the warner
I am the tie that binds
As my insides unravel
I am the purpose and the poise
I am the Judge and the gavel
I am standing alone in a field
Trying to be a normal person
Thoroughly unfulfilled
Judgement is the day that comes
Unwanted

Love Ballad

[Him]: "Yeah, I'm such an easy runner."
[Her]: "So let's head out South for the Summer."
[Him]: "We will have all in your own way."
[Her]: "I'll give you half of what you say."

[Chorus Together]:
"Oooo... I got a line on you."
"Oooo... I got a line on you."

[Him]: "All these towns are so breezy."
[Her]: "Loving this life that's so easy."
[Him]: "Waxing up roses and dining."
[Her]: "It's all about patience and timing."

[Chorus Together]:
"Oooo... I got a line on you."
"Oooo... I got a line on you."
[Bridge Together]
"Every night we can end so tight."
"Reach the wheel and duck into the lights."
"Neon colors streaking by us so fast."
"How much higher can this higher much last?"
"It's Heaven or bust."
"Because..."
"Each of us must..."
"Get back home."

[Chorus Together]:
"Oooo... I got a line on you."
"Oooo... I got a line on you."

[Him]: "I just got shot; it's a bummer."
[Her]: "But all this cocaine is a wonder."
[Him]: "I'm getting cold and it's lonely."
[Her]: "I'll make the most of our money."

[Chorus Together]:
"Oooo… I got a line on you."
"Oooo… I got a line on you."

[Chorus Together]:
"Oooo… I got a line on you."
"Oooo… I got a line on you."

Mannequin Pyre

Imagine you're a mannequin
Deception in the simile
But if you're not real
And I'm not real
Then what are we?

Let's run around the House
Looking for escape inside a Room
Let's cavort around our lives
Wasting feelings 'till we die

Mannequin Pyre
Mannequin Pyre
Set me on fire
Set me on fire
Set me on fire

Experience is nonplussed
For that we make a stormy fuss
But the Other Side
Is unbeknownst
To plastic Fools like us

Let's run around the House
Looking for escape inside a Room
Let's cavort around our lives
Wasting pieces 'till we die

Mannequin Pyre
Mannequin Pyre
Set me on fire
Set you on fire
Set us on fire

Maybe Just A Hat

Maybe this
Or maybe that
Maybe you will wear a hat
Maybe you'll go out today
Maybe you'll cavort or play
Maybe you will lounge about
Or kiss a fool and make him pout
Maybe you will hurt yourself
Or maybe pain somebody else
Maybe you will dwell in silence
Maybe you will savor violence
Maybe you'll find love or loss
Maybe you'll remember
How all things bear a cost
Maybe you will own your choices
Maybe you will share your voices
Maybe you will wear a hat
Nothing else
Just maybe that

Memories

I know
The taste of Moonlight
I know
Day turns into Night
Into memories
Into memories

Memories
Into memories
The tattered photograph was just another connection
Contained within memories

Walking through the forest where the shadows play
The fairy motes lilt away
Into memories
Listen to the music of a regular Day
The hair will dance
The lace will sway
The notes in all gingerly display
Into memories
Memories
Into memories

Misanthrope

One
Twelve
Red
Black
Go
Combinations
Lists and codes
They keep me sane
And in the know

But no one knows
It's in myself
And it's alive
And it's alive

Damn people
Control my life
I say damn them all
Damn them all

No people control my life
I say damn them
Damn them all

I am needing no advice
To survive the Fall
I say damn them all

Nobody will cry for me
After I must go
I say damn them all

Nobody will cry for me
I absolve them all
I say damn their soul

Nobody will cry for me
I don't need your soul
I say damn them all

No torture was spared for me
After I was born
I say damn them all

Misty Sweet and Stolen Memories

A time to forget
Alcohol and cigarettes
Whatever is your best bet
Of the way we were

Misty sweet and stolen memories
Of a time forgotten by time
What is mine

Memories
The times of your choosing
A world of perusing
Of the way we were

Misty sweet and stolen memories
Of a time forgotten by time
What is mine

If we had to do it all again
Would we choose to bear the cost?
Knowing now what time again
Has lost

Mother

Spring blossoms
And shortened sleeves
Summer gardens
Petals and earth
Autumn breezes
And restless leaves
Winter bluster
Comfort in dearth
My Mother's ear
There when I need
My Mother's love
There since my birth

Mushroom Flower Moss

Cultivating madness
Just like Gabby Ray
Sifting through the ashes
The remains of the day

Mushroom
Flower
Moss
Sadness
Love
Loss

Are these dreams for real?
Because they seem so real
And time is like a bullet and a brick

Mushroom
Flower
Moss
Sadness
Love
Loss

The buzzards above
Relish their name
They navigate for spoiled meat
They care nothing for the pain

Mushroom
Flower
Moss
Sadness
Love
Loss

Azariah coldly waits for me
Just beyond the grave
Possibilities would that she'd been made
And instead of pain
I would experience life again
Perhaps that is Hell

Needless Waste

Forge the fire
Wage the the fragile wind
Toil the sallow soil
Pull the Pinyon Pines
And burn the oil
Burn the oil

I can never become who I am

Branch the mighty breach
Foil the fallow heed
Torch the tragic leaves
And toss the seeds
Toss the seeds

I can never become who I am

How blooms misery?
With howling guns
In distant Eaves
How can all this be?
With you and me
In distant dreams

Galvanize the grease
Politic the paste
Wallowing the weak
In needless waste
In needless waste

I can never become who I am

Neptune's Whore

Humanity's soured seed
Washing over the bloom
Of a beautiful flower
Something that is life
Something that bears life
Something that spreads life
Aimlessly engulfing the crevices of its petals
Mingling with the dew
Savagely plowing forward
And stinking the stank
Of Neptune's whore

Never Ever You

Love
Light on the evening air
Love
Is reckless and warm down there
Love
We had the whole affair
Love
Never a single care
Love
Born on the souls of other loves
We had it all
We had it all
Love

Love
Light as an evening breeze
Love
Gone with a single sneeze
Love
It's such a simple game
Love
We turned it all to blame
Love
It took our love to take it all away
We made it work
We made it worse
Love

Darkness
And never
Ever
You

Nibble

You look very adorable
Naked
Lying on your stomach
Arms curled up
Your butt cheeks wiggle
As you giggle
I want to squish them
Nibble them
I mean bite
Okay
I mean bite and nibble
And kiss
And lick
And nibble
And bite
And knead
And moan
The backs of your knees
Licking
And kissing
And massaging
Knees of a Goddess
Made to worship
Holding your gorgeous legs
Kissing you there
Reaching
Groping
For the Heaven

Nihrain

Swift as the ebony wind beneath the stars
Softer her hooves fall in the hard cold rain
Swift Nihrain
Swift Nihrain
Swift Nihrain

Away from the blood-soaked silt of the wars
Black velvet smoke flows the length of her mane
Sweet Nihrain
Sweet Nihrain
Sweet Nihrain

Unreachable hills where the sun dies hard
She gallops far from the bold and the lame
Dark Nihrain
Dark Nihrain
Dark Nihrain

No Endless Home

Today is the day that brings it closer to another
Today is the day that sends it farther from another
Today is the portion of your life that bleeds awareness
The other portion was
Is
And will be
When you were in the timeless

No darkened sky
No cobbled path
No ray of light
No pit of wrath
No Gate of Gates
No wretched wait
No columned stone
No endless home
No endless home

Old Brown River

The trash collection
Is at my door
The trash collection
Is at my door
Old Great River still receding ever more
The trash collection
Is at my door

Old Brown River
Take some more

The trash collection is at my door
And it's bumming me out some more
Because I know
Somehow
Somewhere
Some way
I'll be on that trash heap some day

Old Brown River
Take some more

Opulence

Shiny baubles
Conceal brazen shame
Those without will or whim
Those without name

Come together with me now
Make your stand now
Make it somehow

Tiny bubbles
In Champagne
Make your fist known
Make your own name

Come together with me now
Make your stand now
Make it somehow

Past the wretches
Past the campaign
Past the lunch lines
Past the damp rain
Make it known

Our Game

I'm sad I've drawn you into this smart-edged crap
It's an idiot's game
That should make you laugh
If you weren't so busy crying
I made you cry

Love's in play in our game
Our game
Love's at stake in our game
Our game

I'm glad you've drawn me into your heartfelt gap
It's a lover's game
That should make you cry
If I weren't so busy laughing
You made me laugh

Love's at stake in our game
Our game
Love's in play in our game
Our game

Our Murderous Return

Dabbling your digits in the doldrums of reality
O this magic dream
Orchestrate the values in our emotional poverty
O this seemly dream
Complicate the fires of the Body Politic Elite
O this burning dream
On and on this temperature will rise

The joke we make
The yoke we take
That won't resolve the crime
Just grab a spear
Poke anywhere
Leave Jack Benny's eyes behind

Well you hear them on the road
And you hear them on the street
The Humans that I know are their own dead meat
With a Killer on the road
With a Killer on the street
With a Killer on the road
They're their own dead meat
There's a Killer on the road
There's a Killer on the street
There's a Killer on the road
And they're all dead meat
Dead meat
Dead meat

Come on Baby
I just want to kill you tonight
Running down the alley
Run Baby
Run
Your burning legs trying to beat the smile on this truck

It's gonna ram right through you
That's when I turn the gas on full
Your headlight eyes give me the last glimpse
And the last pleasure
Your deadlight eyes

City lights are bleeding hard tonight
You see
That's the cutoff line
I was just waving you by
So let it ride
Baby
Bye-bye

Outside the Realm of Nature

You look nice
I look like a monster
Nobody has stared through these eyes before
Into the mirror
I look like a prick who likes flicking bitches' tits
What is your desire?
What is your sickness?
I'll fuck your pretty little face

Sometimes I see wildlife
Strolling through the foliage
They've lost some of the fear that makes them wild
Here amongst the trees and houses
But I fear everything and nothing
I'm so civilized I could die
I have everything and nothing
I startle at a sudden movement
I panic at a single noise
Inside me I squirm and rant
But I am pleasant as a Pheasant
When I'm gazing at your little fuckable face

I often want to die
To be swallowed into blackness
But I'm afraid to do the deed
I'm afraid of failure
So I stare into the mirror and hate and love what I see
How do I work my fear into something pure?
I long for some abuse
And for someone to abuse

Chores are tedious and banal
They are outside the realm of Nature
I am a Whore and a Princess
An unnatural work of order

I long to be trussed up and pampered
I want my insides on the outside
I want to be a Stag and a Fawn
A Fag and a Pawn
I want someone to fuck my pretty little face
And hold me when they're done
There is something so unnatural
About being alone

Patterns

I've been long long
Long long gone
Wrong wrong
Wrong
Wrong
Wrong
I've been long long
Long long gone

I've been pale and pasty
Sudden and hasty
And long long
Long long gone

Patterns can be cool
Patterns breed a Fool
Patterns get emboldened
Patterns can leave you broken

I've been fat and lazy
Harried and crazy
And wrong wrong
Wrong
Wrong
Wrong

Patterns can be cool
Patterns breed a Fool
Patterns get emboldened
Patterns can leave you broken

Let me cut to the chase
Let me carve through the waste
Let me get strong strong

Strong
Strong
Strong

I've been long long
Long long gone
Wrong wrong
Wrong
Wrong
Wrong
Let me get strong strong
Strong
Strong
Strong

Persistence

Wisps of white grey smoke
Playing with the lonely breeze
Out breathe in breathe out

Numbers mark the day
And this is how we span Time
Span Time together

Motivated deeds
In a dry and weary way
Cast call for the Dead

Waterfalls and flows
Trickling and thunderous
Wearing down the Past

Foliage flaring
Beasts and birds and insects thrive
And pass with the Dawn

Time now Time unknown
Tumultuous it passes
The Chessboard of Time

As I Live I Die
The pencil draws erasures
Holographic art

Wisps of white grey smoke
Playing with the lonely breeze
Out breathe in breathe out

Pin Stripe Boys

Keep your hat on
Don't miss the mark
Keep tumbling
Don't *Jump the Shark*
Lay down your bets
And play to win
And keep your hat on
Don't sweat the spin

Pin Stripe Boys are here to win

Keep your feet down
Not up and out
Pump your fist around
Just jump and shout
Slick your hair back
And bend your knees
Keep your feet down
And clip *The Squeeze*

Pin Stripe Boys do not say please

Keep your hat on
Don't miss the mark
Keep tumbling
Don't *Jump the Shark*
Cash your chips in
And make your move
And keep your shirt loose
Just *Cut the Groove*

Pin Stripe Boys are on the move

Pleasure Games

The need to feed
On space and speed
On slashing
And grabbing
And mashing
And stabbing
On blinking lights
And city heights
Man get tight
This is gonna ride all night

The need to feed
On what you need
On what you think
Your body needs
Consume yourself
Chew up your limbs
It's only meat
Fatted meat
So sumptuous
And that's the high you are looking for

Psychosis Heatscape

Yep
I was in a grape once but never did
I was in a flower and then another flower
Then I was…
Hey look I know you Turkey
Die
Die
He says it so much I know we're not going to die
Die
Die
We can't have this stuff
Give back
Coffee must be hell
Ha
Ha
Ha
Ha
Ha
We're done

You know our Leader that crazy Guy
Yeah
I know Him
He doesn't do anything
Until he bangs
Bangs
We used to go down to Vera's Baubles and I didn't like it
I've got the Mad and this Grey is on me
I still won't get ahead where I'm going
Chicken on the Orange
We still have another One and another Thing growing
The background surface heat is all that matters

Broken your fist arm and broken your Second
I'd like to go out and kill your Old Man
You're a Red Eye on a sandwich bag handkerchief
Shut yourself down
Get out of my way

I am a Man
I am a Madman
I can stare right into your eyes
You will never turn me
You will never understand me
O you want to talk about it
To share the better sights you've seen
It's getting sober and a little bit closer
Drink it
Drink it
Drink it
You can do better
He's definitely praying now

These conversations
These interrogations
In the South about a deep red grotto
Been missing from a discovered object
There's a Man on the Moon
There's a Man on the Moon
Yes indeed
And if you know it don't forget it
Because it all goes back Someday
We all go back Someday
March in the Ceremony of Rags

Is that what you are afraid of
Watching this old wicked World burn?
It's been burning every day
Since the beginning of Time

Today we ride to Town
To take those People down
Hoot and holler
Hoot and holler
Raise the Cross and raise the Dead
We don't care much what Jesus said
We just hoot and holler
And tighten the collar

Quest

Questioning your life
Visiting your mind
Investigating why
Things are the way they are

Mired in the journey
Imitating what you see
Never will you grow to know
Everyone with Love

Knowing is to be uncertain
Reason is to face unknowns
Any heart can beat for certain
But lonely hearts can beat alone

Quiet Riot

Edge of the night
Come following
Edge of a knife
Come flowing

You are always the last one to go
As you go wandering the show
You are always the last one to know
As your mind shuffles through snow

And it's a long way down
Roses fall apart
And it's a long way down
Roses fall apart

You welcome all the carnage on the street
Are witness to the processing of meat
Sticks and stones may break my bones
But your mind breaks waves when you're alone

And at the edge of the throng
All the Prophets of Doom
Come calling
Calling
And it's a long way down
Calling
It's always a long way down
To The End

Raindrops and Diamonds

Dollops of raindrops
Cascading from the sky
They gleam like diamonds
In the intermittent light
And then I gaze into your eyes
Raindrops and diamonds

We resonate with ancient rhythms
Our basic inclinations
Fascination grips us
And buries its pleasure seed
Elegant and primitive

Delicate fumbling
Hot breath on my shoulder
Sweat beads like diamonds
On the surface of your skin
And then I touch them with my tongue
Raindrops and diamonds

Red

Red
Red that makes you feel that you are best
Red that views you better off as dead
Lording that it isn't funk (pink)
White and blue are just a heavy junk (stink)
Red glares at them and just kind of winks

White
White that's not so fond of red and blue
White that thinks it's best for me and you
Thinking what is of the greater fix
White would rather us not pick up sticks
White that knows how time may be a mix

Blue
Blue that thinks it knows of me and you
Blue that feels it knows it has a clue
Lording over that it isn't Green
Who knows what the fact that really means?
Blue that someday hopes that we will see

Or our will

Redneck Rhapsody

Johnny's in the pig pen
Sloppin' up a sow
C'mon Son
Deliver it up now
Deliver up those pork rinds

Comfort food for all Boy!
Comfort food for all!
(Da-Da-Da-alotalot-Do-Da-Hoo)
I was born in Tallahassee
Okla-Alabamee

We got Fred and Tate and Cletus and Skeeter
Marge is on the stone pipe working the feeder

Would you like that?
Well I bet you would
Cotton and the grain corn
Choppin' up wood
And tearing up the town

Comfort food for all Boy!
Comfort food for all!
(Da-Da-Da-alotalot-Do-Da-Hoo)
I was born in Tallahassee
Okla-Alabamee

We got Fred and Tate and Cletus and Skeeter
Marge is on the stone pipe working the feeder

C'mon Jim
Step on down
Please step on down
Now c'mon Boy
Now c'mon Son

Comfort food for all Boy!
Comfort food for all!
(Da-Da-Da-alotalot-Do-Da-Hoo)
I was born in Tallahassee
Okla-Alabamee

We got Fred and Tate and Cletus and Skeeter
Marge is on the stone pipe working the feeder

Telling stories
Chewing chaw
Telling stories
Chewing chaw
Hey what's up with that chaw-cholker?
Hey what's up with that chaw-cholker?
Wonder if he'll howl for mercy
As we take our pleasure
Hey what's up with that chaw-cholker?
Hey what's up with that chaw-cholker?
Have his tax return sent to us
We'll clean his engine

Stick that nugget in him
As we put some perks in him

We got Fred and Tate and Cletus and Skeeter
Marge is on the stone pipe working the feeder

Comfort food for all Boy!
Comfort food for all!
(Da-Da-Da-alotalot-Do-Da-Hoo)
I was born in Tallahassee
Okla-Alabamee

Reverend Mother in the House of Angels

My hands are looking old
Water was the sound that I made in my throat
Morbid stories bold unfold
I hold my breath

Revered Mother
In the House of Angels

You breathe lips to mouth
Towels were the means to stifle the screams
Tears flow proud and loud
I wipe them away

Revered Mother
In the House of Angels

I'm inside you now
Fear was a trope they related in fables
Displacing what was pain
I love you

Revered Mother
In the House of Angels

Run

Who are you now?
Who do you want to be?
Is it just a dream?
Run

What are your weights?
What is bringing you down?
Can you shed them off?
Can you run?

How is this working out?
Are you afraid to be free?
Do you fear what will be?
Run

Run into the Sea
How far can you run?

Sapphire in a Storm

Beaded dew on sanguine rose
Curtain lace on fervent breeze
Desert thoughts in languid throes
Leaves in chorus through ancient trees
Play upon the soul
A sapphire in a storm

Scamper and Scurry

Scampering
Chasing products
Consumerism
Good
Bad
What's the difference?

Having time
Or thinking you do
You scurry
You plan
You store away nuts

Not having time
Everything becomes simple
You enjoy the day
You make what may
You expend your nuts

There is no shame
In your game
Unless the crimes you play
Are yours to blame
Of course you'll pay

Scamper and scurry
Little busy hurriers
Don't you worry
Good
Bad
What's the difference?

Scorpio Chasing Gemini

October embers brush out the day
The breezes stir up their dalliance
Footsteps on a path less traveled
A capricious laugh
The shadows dance

And there you were
A constant whisper in my mind
Secrets of a lost desire
That was fire
Fire

The skies turn ash when I summon your name
But your smile is a child
And your eyes blaze wild
Nesting branches
And savage lances

Pour the wine
And stoke the pyres
Leaves transcend the dawn today
The sky invokes its ire
But you are there within me now
And you are fire

Strange that I can hold you now
And taste your perspiration
Salty tears and liquid dreams
Heat and hesitation
And then sensation
Elation

Scorpio chasing Gemini

Scratch

At first it's a scratch
You apply the salve
Not a scar
Just a scratch
And nothing more

Scratches build up to form wounds
Easily bandaged
Just a scar
A healed-up wound
And nothing more

Wounds build up to form trauma
Gaping holes
Major damage
Suturing
And nothing more

Trauma becomes fatality
Limbs are compromised
Lives extinguished
Forgotten lives
And nothing more

And then you move on
And then things move on
It all leads to a whimper
It all leads to a whisper
And nothing more

Self-Discovery

Candle sticks
And candle wicks
With flicker flicks
Then candle stops
You're gonna piss and moan
When candle pops
But living in your head is such a boring mess
You're gonna find a World when you get dressed
Your faith gets lost
And time is stopped
Your heart reverses
And rots
Time to discover yourself anew

Social Tension

A badge and a gun
Niggers on the run
Niggers with no sense of worth

All said and done
You've had your fun
All born and dead of the Earth

Hold the child of all colors
Tame the wild of all colors
Feel the mild in all colors
Share a smile with all colors

Man of the mask
Batons and gas
What instinct came to pass?

Now lives are changed
So rearranged
Now there is another birth

Hold the child of all colors
Tame the wild of all colors
Feel the mild in all colors
Share a smile with all colors

Share a smile with all colors

So It Begins

Lips
Curling
Trembling
Lusty sickness
Anticipation
Mashing against another pair
Tongues
Thrusting
Snaking for purchase
Hands
Groping
Petting
Eager and greedy
Bodies
Shifting
Pushing
Grinding
So it begins

Something from Nothing

You've got a few more years to ramble and babble
You've got a tower up to Heaven made of toothpicks and scrabble
When the stars bleed out and empty the sky
Even your name can die
Even your name can die

Your talk is full of something that knows nothing from nothing
Your faith is in the gutter where your love becomes fear
When happiness smears its hand across your smug face
It's the last place
It's the last place

We are all alive inside ourselves
And nobody likes our hair
When will someone infiltrate?
And cause all despair
We moan about our tragic lives
We whine about our wares
But no one really gives a shit
Because no one really cares

When the stars bleed out and empty the sky
Even time can die
Even time can die

Spiral

A spoiled Nation rants and raves
She brought to me a bottle of Bourbon
And told me to behave
Told me to be brave

Now I'm getting closer to the never
Forever
Now I'm getting closer to the never
Forever

Around the way
You'll see their faces
Tree bound with ropes and leathers
Buried in a Bible
Discarded in the Heather
Way down deep in notes and letters

Around the way
You'll see their faces
Around the way
To the never
Forever

Steam

I've had no pleasure
Like this river of emotion
Like water meeting air
Air descending deep into the ocean's depths
Into lakes and rivulets
Flowing where the liquid roams
Or cuddling in a lonely puddle
Joining into H2O
And floating
Ascending upwards towards the Sun
A perennial Icarus
To drift
To fly
To touch the fire
To embrace the flame
To wander through the labyrinth of the Infinite
If only for a brief sojourn
You are there
Because you are in here
Searching for what is already known

The fire
The inextinguishable fire
The ocean
The seamless surging ocean
The steam
The glorious billowing steam
Aching to merge with the air
Urging ever upwards
To the limitless sky
The pairs converge
To form something new from what they are

Learning flight
Embracing light
Yearning to mingle
With the deep embers glowing lonely in the night
Warm and moist
Fluid and transient
We learn to dance
We learn to pleasurably collide
You and I

Stump

I know you are honest
Because I don't know what you said
I know you are honest
Because I know that's what you said

And I hope you like insurance
Because I hope you like your meds

Stump
Stump
We all get trumped
Stump
Stump
We all fall down

Here's a tiny favor
And I hope you will oblige
Make somebody pay for
What is coming out inside

And I hope you like insurance
Because I hope you like your meds

Stump
Stump
We all get trumped
Stump
Stump
We all fall down

And I hope you like your wasteland
Because I hope you like your fear
So drink up all your whiskey
And follow it with beer

And I hope you like insurance
Because I hope you like your meds

Stump
Stump
We all get trumped
Stump
Stump
We all fall down

Jobs and jobs and jobs and jobs
And jobs and jobs and jobs
Work your fingers to the bone
Because soon you will get robbed

And I hope you like insurance
Because I hope you like your meds

Stump
Stump
We all get trumped
Stump
Stump
We all fall down

And I hope you like your army
Because I hope you like your bed
Because one becomes the other
And it's you who end up dead

And I hope you like insurance
Because I hope you like your meds

Stump
Stump
We all get trumped
Stump
Stump
We all fall down

We all fall down
We all fall down
Come Hell or high water
We all fall down

We all get stumped
When we all get trumped
We all fall down

Subterfuge

I feel the cold sickness baking off of me in a constant wave
They sense nothing
How is it not reaching them?
It should be smashing them like ocean tides
Still they talk incessantly about transient concerns
I'm drifting away
Not my attention
Nor my calculated expressions
Nor my magnanimous answers
But myself
My self
Is drifting away

Sure

Sure the fuzzy music just got crushed
And my mind a mobile unit ain't enough
The city is a black wash yellow dots
Bending through the straight of parking lots

Where is the mean in meaningless?
Speaking God's words speaks the Devil's?
Would you know the pathway to Hell?
What if that pathway led you here?

What you don't think is right
Is your right not to think
Engage me in an argument
That leads me back into your mind
Reverse it when you are about to die

Muck and mush and slushy fuss
The cobwebs melt like ice flakes in our open palms
Your fingers clasp a conduit
To the sorrow of an empty soul

Survivor

Nobody answers me
Nobody answers
Lost in their own little lives
Nobody answers

I am a cancer
I am avoided
I'm not the answer
And I am annoyed

Best to take the medication
But maybe you should just jump
Getting to the answer is a worthy pursuit
For what it is worth

What formulates the feeling?
What mollifies the meaning?
What saturates the stealing?
Of a good life

Even though you aren't with me
Or near me
I have survived all of my living years

Thank You for Touching Me

It is true and we are
Disillusion from afar
I can still see the yawning chasm
Growing before our vision
As we drive headlong towards it in our car

I thought my life was going to end
I thought my life was going to end
And it did
And it did
Thank you for touching me

Reserves to be drawn
Living on my own
I've never been alone before
Except in pretend
And now pretend is for real

Periods of disbelief so profound
Another week went by
Another week went by
Another week goes by
And we're still here

I thought my life was going to end
I thought my life was going to end
And it did
And it did
Thank you for touching me

I dug you out of the chasms of my heart
None of this was supposed to happen
Forever… and such fairy tales
Reduced to scraps and stories and remains
All those unforgiven sleights

Slowly we untether
Red balloons careening into the sky
Separating indefinitely
And casually saying goodbye
And somehow we did not die

I thought my life was going to end
I thought my life was going to end
And it did
And it did
Thank you for touching me

Nothing left to give
Nothing left to take
No glue to bind us together anymore
Consuming each other
Until there was nothing left to consume

And now it's Closing Time
Beginning again from another beginning's end
Thank you for touching me
Hope everything is going well on your side of life
As such… our memories remain

That Dance

That stance
That sway
That swagger
That play

Issuance
That stare
Curious
So fair

That dance
That fray
That power
That play

Insurance
From trust
Your hair
My lust

That stance
That sway
That swagger
That play

Patience
A must
Your lace
Your bust

That dance
That fray
That power
That play

Tiger claws
Down pelt
Neck nibble
Tongues and sweat

That stance
That sway
That swagger
That play

Things get hard
Things get soft
Empathy
And innocence lost

That dance
That fray
That power
That play

Cumming
Inside
All flesh
No pride

And we are cumming
Cumming inside

That Darkness

That darkness in the hall
That darkness in the hall
That shape
Dark shape
That darkness in the hall

Window
Mirror
You are there
You are there
Window
Mirror
You are there
You are there

That darkness in the hall
That darkness in the hall
That shape
Dark shape
That darkness in the hall

Shape and shade
Sweat stained skin
Who is here?
Who is here?
Twisted dreams
Saturnines
Who is here?
Who is here?

That darkness in the hall
That darkness in the hall
That shape
Dark shape
That darkness in the hall

In the hall
Someone there
In the doorway
Someone there
In my bedroom
Someone there

I'm not here

The Big Crush

The water just keeps on rolling in
Big fat tunneling tides
Striking the rocks of the shore
Breaking apart
Thick strands of milky white foam
Aquamarine undertones

Way out
As far as the eye can discern
The blue sky greets the Sea
Fading to hazy yellow tinged white
There
Out there is nothing
Just the incomparable incomprehensible mass
The undulating rippling tides

Casual seagulls
Sun parched timeless stone
The never-ending spectacle
Rhythm and peace
The Sun goes down
The Ocean changes
The Sky becomes a masterpiece
Infinite grace

It was larger once
I can see it in the hills
Over time

The Cave

Pacific Northwest air is churning
Weaving through the laden forests
Caressing the ever-errant strangers
Everywhere
As only it can do

The Mystic Warriors exit the Cave
The fires burned
The chants sounded
The rituals played
For a better day

With granite faces
They measure their paces
Greeting with no remembrance
The snowy brightness
The forest shining

The water trickles
Everywhere
Movement and music
Everywhere
All of the unknowns
Everywhere
The whole World
Everywhere
Everything
Everywhere

The Mystic Warriors stiffen their pace
And merge into the mists
When the great fires fade
Consuming all we bore witness to
The countless flames from endless Heavens

Geared for fear
The Frat Boys with their ballroom blather
Guzzle the ancient fermentations
As they cavort and lumber around the blazing bonfire
Hazing their indifference to the World

We will watch their signals
And we will share wisdom
Light connects us all

The Fountain & The Fire

They haven't been recessed
On account of the rain
Now they are searing
With the pleasure of pain
What is practical and obvious

When you love someone
You love the entire
The Fountain & The Fire

There are tombstones in his eyes
And still he longs to lie
Within the longing
Where ghosts come alive
Something's wrong with Time

When you love someone
You drown in desire
The Fountain & The Fire

What is a test but a test of pain?
What is the Ocean but a collection of rain?
And what is fire without the fuel?
The whispering flickers
The scintillating pools

When you love someone
You love the entire
The Fountain & The Fire

I came for you
We came for each other
Familiar strangers
Perennial lovers
Shadows under covers

When you love someone
You drown in desire
The Fountain & The Fire

I could cry forever in your arms
When I die I want to be there staring in your eyes
Maybe I will see what you see
Maybe we will come unglued
Maybe you will take me there with you

The Fountain & The Fire

The Gathering

The clouds gathered across the plains
Long and low
Billowing
Dark and brooding they became
With whispers of rain

The Bison roamed across the plains
Large and slow
Fallowing
Stark and skittish they became
With nothing to reign

The boots of Men compressed the plains
Reap and sow
Harrowing
Stout and sturdy they became
With bellows of rage

The Killing Joke

Ambulate
Anemic mate
Show me how to demonstrate
Ambulate
From shade to shape
Show me how to compensate

Too much batshit going on
It's a sad affair
But not enough to care
When your memories know I'm gone
Not a lot to touch
Not that nothing's much

I do
I really really
Love you

Too much catfish want a prawn
Too much fantasy
Too much more for me
Too much not to know I'm wrong
No embarrassment
No more feelings spent

Too much bitching on the phone
Too much points to make
Too much "made mistakes"
Too much you is not your own
You forget the price
You sing "Edelweiss"

I do
I really really
Love you

Too much Roosters on the bong
Too much ink to stretch
Too much quick success
Every crooner sings a song
Every bloke's a throat
In the Killing Joke

The Last Day

I'm gonna make it to The Last Day
The Last Day is gonna follow me
I'm gonna make it to The Last Day
The Last Day is gonna set me free

FINANCIALS
EMISSIONS
OFFICIALS
SUSPICIONS

Someone's gonna follow me

SPATIAL
PALATIAL
RACIAL
And FACIAL

Someone's gonna follow me
For sure

I'm gonna make it to The Last Day
The Last Day is gonna follow me
I'm gonna make it to The Last Day
The Last Day is gonna set me free

GROUNDED
And POUNDED
No known WHISTLE
Ever SOUNDED

Someone's gonna follow me

BAITING
And HATING
All HOPE
Is FADING

Someone's gonna follow me
For sure

I'm gonna make it to The Last Day
The Last Day is gonna follow me
I'm gonna make it to The Last Day
The Last Day is gonna set me free

I've got your NUMBER
Smashed inside your Death Bed lumber
No time to slumber
Gas in a Can
You know who I Am

The Last Page

Here we are
Interconnected
Someone died
We are still alive
With one less connection to bind us

Trees imbue the breath of death in the Fall
They are beautiful as the leaves change hues
We should use that muse
In the breath of us all
Death belies growth

I knew a Man standing in fields unknown
Every move a choice
I believe in things lost and found
Every soul a voice
We are here and we are now
And we can share a time
It may mean something else someday
But right now
It is yours
And it is mine

The Light of Your Eyes

In the final moment
When the light goes out from your eyes
What will you have been?
What will you have seen?
What will you have done?
What will you have given?
What will you have said?
What will you have forgotten?
What will you have destroyed?
What will you have turned away from?
What will you have passed by?
What will you have taken?
What will you have squandered?
What will you have found?
And who will know it?
In that final moment
When the light goes out from your eyes

The Madman's Lament

The little girl backwards
Me dancing backwards
The Spring blossoms backwards
Me dancing backwards

Who am I what am I?
What am I who am I?

The snow falling backwards
Me skipping backwards
The leaves falling backwards
Me skipping backwards

What am I who am I?
Who am I what am I?

The Sun shining backwards
Me walking backwards
The Sea rolling backwards
Me walking backwards

Who am I what am I?
What am I who am I?

As I grow I am stolen
The falling snow
The restless leaves
As I grow I am stolen
The shining Sun
The groaning Sea
As I grow I am stolen
The backwards girl
The dancing me
As I grow I am stolen
The Spring blossoms backwards

The Man in the Clouds

There He is
The Man in the Clouds
Stroking His perfect beard
And talking silently loud
Somebody thinks they hear Him
And they tell you what they think He says
But nobody ever answers
Save the grave

Look at Him now
The Man with the Plan
Thousands of years were painted
Looking perfectly grand
Love was a simple answer
But turned to power play
Mankind seems to like it
That way

Look at you now
A toddler Tot
Nodding your head to something
Someone tells you is not
You never had an answer
And you never had a choice
Millions of children
Following the Voice

The Marvel Men

When metal fades and magic dims
Darkness claims the Marvel Men
But baubles bright besiege the eyes
They crave to see the light

With Pick in hand and Dagger blade
We mine the ore for what we've made
Smelting
Molding
Brass and gold
For wheels and cogs
And bearings bold

While clouds and Dragons skim the sky
Over Elves and Dwarves and Giant-kind
And Men who dwell in fabled halls
Beneath we dwell unseen by all

Here under the common soil
Winches pull and Tinkers toil
Here devices brought to life
Share the metal and the might

The Marvel Men create desires
Spears and spokes and copper wires
Anything the Heart inspires
From the forge and from the fire

The Movement in the Light

Clean edges
Nice designs
Straight lines
Blurred lives

These things
Gas and light and dust
Elements and tension
To what purpose?
To what must?

Some answer in the wind
Within the waves and magma
The constant churn
No quarter

Something special
No empathy
We are all stupid animals
Vying for power

In a thousand years
In a thousand says
Someone will show us
Who we are
But we won't notice
And life goes on

It's like the Ocean
And it's like the breeze
Sweet life
Come with me

How things will destroy
How things will return
How things will become
How things will burn

The selfishness of nature
That certain passage
That open door
Water changes everything

Radiance
Painful radiance
What you and I do not know and yet we know
The moment in the Light

The Performer

Screw
Screw
Turn the screw

Hammer
Nail
Wall will fail

White heat
White sheets
Spilled drinks
Musty stink
Turn seams
Fumblings
Fast crest
Fast mess

Now you're the Performer
Beating off in the corner
No one could know her
So you stroke in her honor
And she laughs
And she laughs
And she laughs

The wind whispers misery
And you cry all alone
To a dangling phone

The Race

I'm not a poster baby
I'm not a toaster baby
I'm not a roaster baby or a can

I'm not an order baby
I'm not a sorter baby
I'm not a penis or a Pawn

Spit your fire at me
Don't want to be your Daddy
If you're a runner baby
I'm gonna give you a race

Maybe a child baby
Maybe a Secret Lady
Maybe no good or no fun

But I'm no "hum" or "maybe"
I like my cheese and gravy
And I'm gonna burn like the Sun

Spit my cum back at me
Don't want to be your Daddy
If you're a runner baby
I'm gonna give you a race

I'm gonna spit in your face

The Rainy Season

My body is alive
Upon my back
My body is buoyed upon the temperate, undulating, lilting blue
My hair splays out in a sodden halo around my head
Beads of perspiration dapple my brow in the humid air
My eyes shimmer with tears in the fathomless sky
Moisture tickles my lips with fickle kisses
The sharing of fluids
My breath is deep, sultry, and damp
Caressing my throat and tongue as it mingles amongst the Sea within
And the Ocean without
And at last my watery Lover comes
Not as a dark embrace from the cold depths below
But as a weightless white Angel floating fluidly above
Laden with the grey sorrows of change and time
Shifting and dancing, her face forms there
And she weeps of the Rainy Season upon my soaked frame
My body is purified
My mind is cleansed
My soul is refreshed
My senses are fluid
And she passes on
My body is alive

The Repetitiveness of Things

You say something
Then you say something else
Suddenly the temperature is starting to turn
You reach out your hand for something to burn
And every moment a thought will churn
And you will go on your way

I'm trapped in a wheel inside a wheel
I feel I can't get out
The shadow that chases me is real
But I'm dealing with doubt
Roses fall apart
Roses fall apart

You were my World
Then you stoked my shame
Then you shone as hope
Then you imbued pain
I would agonize over the repetitiveness of things
And then return to the repetitiveness of things

There is Sun
And there is sky
I don't know why
I don't know why
You say something
Then you say something else

The Road

That wet road
Looks like glass
Like a mirror
Everything bleeding into everything else
A hot mess
A hot mess

Dotted lines and lights
Measure without end
Everything bleeding into everything else

That wet road looks like glass like a mirror
Everything bleeding into everything else
A hot mess a hot mess

Dotted lines and lights measure without end
Everything bleeding into everything else

That wet road looks like glass like a mirror
Everything bleeding into everything else
A hot mess a hot mess

Dotted lines and lights measure without end everything bleeding into
everything else

The Void

Ghostly hue
Rainy day
In the Afternoon
In the Evening

Certain thoughts
Certain thoughts you cannot put into words

Ghostly hue
Winter day
In the Morning
In the Evening

Certain thoughts
Certain thoughts you cannot put into words

Ghostly hue
Summer day
In the Evening
In the Morning

Certain thoughts
Certain thoughts you cannot put into words

Ghostly hue
Eternal shade
In the Void
In the Void

The Vultures

Out in Guerneville
In Western Sonoma County
Yeah
California
I've been surveying the Vultures
The fucking Turkey Vultures
There is a Pack of them here where I live
Or is it a Flock?
Or is it a Murder?
Maybe that's Crows
The Vultures
They hang out
Lusting for lunch
Lurching for love
They land on the rooftops
Perusing the goings on
They land upon the branches
And spread their feathers before the Sun
To be warmed by the Sun
To worship before the Sun
They land upon the Telephone wires
Yes
The Telephone wires
The wires are still above ground in Guerneville
Some call the town "Gurneyville"
(*Laughs ensue*)
But it's Guerneville
And the locals will take issue with your pronunciation
But the Turkey Vultures don't care
They land on the Telephone wires
And they struggle for balance

Why?
Why would they do this?
Why would they intentionally land on wires
And struggle for balance?
For amusement
It amuses them
And they are amused

These Chairs

These chairs
They used to rest on a beach
There was a tent and a mattress
There was sleeping inside and outside
And these chairs

These chairs
They used to rest on a beach
There was a fire and some laughter
There was music from a local channel
And there were these chairs

When I think of our life
I think of these chairs
I dream of the surf
I dream of the fog horn
I dream of the barking Sea Lions
I dream of the Dog sleeping on my lap
I think of the hot dogs cooked by the fire
I dream of the hot whisky buzz
And I think of the nature of things
The sex and the surf
The coming and going
The sand and the fog and the wind
Like a troupe of mystical saviors
And these chairs

These chairs
They rest in my back yard
The party is over
One gathers detritus
And one cradles a Loner
These chairs

These Days

Why this long song?
This drawn page?
Why this cold drab?
This endless stage?
Why this tired news?
This pulled pain?
Why these parched days?
This empty gain?
Why this furtive gaze?
This hard rain?

Sallow hearts
Morose decay
Frigid lives
Harrowing
Callow
Vain

Things That Were Consumed

Things were consumed
Food was consumed
Liquor was consumed
Friends were consumed
Good will was consumed
Lies were consumed
Hate was consumed
Pain was consumed
Bodies were consumed
Blood was consumed
Time was consumed
Love was consumed
Pleasure was consumed
Past was consumed
Present was consumed
Future was consumed

You used to love me so much
You used to love me

We were consumed

This and That

Nobody knows the words that you don't speak
Nobody knows the secrets that you keep
But somebody knows the words that you told them
And somebody knows what you've showed them
And now it's their knowledge to hide or reveal

Many don't want to accept that fact
But this is this and that is that
And whether it rhymes
Or whether it fizzles
Whether it dillies or dallies
Or dithers or drizzles
You know the end is nigh
When no one bats an eye

Today Like No Tomorrow

The hardest thing to reach is peace
Today like no tomorrow
The peace within yourself
The hardest thing to reach

I'm not a Man of words or wisdom
Today like no tomorrow
I am a Man of pure emotion
It leads me where I follow

There is a field in a distant realm
Today like no tomorrow
It is there I see your face
Absent pain or sorrow

Together

Metal to rust
Twigs to ashes
It's going to be the same
To include the best of us
~ *HEB*

From the dust of stars we are born
This is the gateway to our world
Through this door
And whatever come what may
So we too shall pass this way
~ *SEB*

Top of the Cliff

When you are slogging through a bog
And there is no end in sight
When you are feeling out for something
In a cold dark bitter night

When you reach a New Beginning
There's a grey exalted feeling
When you're not sure if you may just might

At the Top of the Cliff
There's a moment that's stiff
There's an avalanche of waiting
It's all going down from here

At the Top of the List
In a memory's whiff
There's an avalanche of waiting
It's all going down from here

When you reach a New Beginning
There's a grey exalted feeling
When think that you just may just might

When you grind through the grist
There's a moment like this
There's an avalanche of waiting
It's all going down from here

When you get to the gist
When you've cleared through the mist
There's an avalanche of waiting
It's all going down from here

When you cut to the chase
Not a moment to waste
There's an avalanche of writing
It's all going down from here

It's all going down
It's all going down from here now

To Mars and Back

I will go all the way to Mars and back
Cold and black
Cold and black
I will go all the way to Mars and back
Just to be with you
Just to be with you

I will meet you at the Event Horizon
Deep and black
Deep and black
I will meet you at the Event Horizon
Through Eternity
Through Eternity

And when the sparkle in your eyes
Fades and dies
Fades and dies
I will be with you
I will be with you

Tussle

Long thoughts
Broad thoughts
Deep thoughts
And what today have you brought me?

Hanky Panky?
Henny Penny?
Play the Fool?
As good as any

Why you wanna axe me like that?
That stain upon your brain
Why you wanna play with that?
The song remains the same

Maybe you want to barter
With your passion and your pain
Maybe you want a cart for
Your barrels full of rain

Simon says
And it be done
Congratulations
You have won

Word to your Brother
Your Sister and your Mother
Word to your Father
He cannot get much larger

Maybe it was fun
Some messed up kind of pun
This tussle we shared

Two Cats

Sproggles is pondering me funny
Like I ain't even real
Like I ain't supposed to be here
Like Cthulhu is emerging from my ears
Tentacles green and submarine
I never slighted that Cat
Bet he's got the upstairs gears
And he's got Magnum style
Spider back
From his radial smile
He's a Black Magic Cat
If you can dig it
So dig it
Even though he's pink and white and grey
Sometimes I am not in his day
Forget it anyways

I spy Monkey in the corner
Bouncing up and down
And all around
Now he's bounding down the corridor
Bouncing off the walls
And ripping down the hall
Man, that Cat is crazy
Googly eyes
And whipping tail
Man, that Cat's bananas
All trumpet blares
Drum beats
And symbol crashes
Maybe a xylophone or two
A saxophone spasm
Man, that Cat is cool

Unasked

Walking on the beach
Reaching for something that is almost out of reach
Lives defy belief
Seeking out beginnings that are ends

Why did it have to be you?
Who walked into the room?
Who walked right through that very room?
And so I followed
I followed

I caught you on the porch
No one knew my Heart would spawn a torch
You gave me what I wanted
And that's the moment I became haunted

Why did it have to be you?
In the wake of that perfume?
I fell into the wake of that perfume
And there I wallowed
I wallowed

Walking on the beach
Reaching for something that is almost out of reach
Lives defy belief
Seeking out beginnings that are ends

Why did it have to be you?
That vagrant smile
That petulant child
The striding of miles
In the mazes of my mind
Formaldehyde in my veins
So that smile in my brain
And that sweet perfume
That sweet perfume

Uncharted Territories

The days flow through Daymares
And time moves away
The rain drops plops into puddles
Which expand into waves

The ivy climbs the tree trunks
To cling to the generous sky
Nights turn into Nightscapes
And you don't wonder why

Dishes adorn the basin
And there's filth upon the floor
Cat hair combs the carpet
Ambivalence eats my core

Taking care of cares
And there is no other end
I crawl into Morning
And it all begins again

Uncharted territories
But water returns to water
And earth returns to earth
Air still feeds the fire
And fire burns
It burns

It is what it is

Universal Ownership

By now you know
We make the rules
We take the rules
We break the rules
We make the rules

By now you know
We make your cash
We take your cash
We break your cash
We make your cash

By now you know
We make your life
We take your life
We break your life
We make your life

By now you know
We're in your head
We take your head
We break your head
We rape your head

Head like a hole
Take your head
Head like a hole
Break your head
Head like a hole
Rape your head
Rape your head
Rape your head

By now you know
We're in your head
Head like a hole
Faceless your mask
Heartless your soul
By now you know

Now you know

Vortex

Things falling
Things falling
Lost lives
Lost lives

Things falling
Things falling
Lost times
Lost minds

Memories fade
Memories die
Memories warped
And twisted with time

How came you to this place?
How came you to this face?
Mirror casts an unknown fate
Perhaps a bit too late

Memories fade
Memories die
Memories warped
And twisted with tide

Things falling
Things falling
Lost times
Lost minds

Things falling
Things falling
Lost loves
Lost lives

Wake Up

Wake up
You're living
I can hear it in your cries
Your face is pink and beautiful
And we're gonna share our lives

Wake up
It's time to play
I hear it in your sighs
Your gait is young and graceful
And we're gonna scale some spires

Wake up
You didn't smile
And you're telling me some lies
And now you've gone and done that thing
The thing that I despise

Wake up
Take this hit
It alleviates your mind
I care not what you crave in life
As long as it is mine

Wake up
You're in control
Of all that is so fine
Enjoy it while it lasts you Fool
For that's the pain of Time

Wake up
You're dreaming
I can see it in your eyes
Your lips are red and sensual
And now we share a smile

Wake up
You're empty
Things are dark and tired
You're mired in the mine again
Of impotence and mild

Wake up
You're ugly
You're morbid rabid mold
Exiting the quiet
They avoid your fog of cold

Wake up
You're dead
You've lived a long good life
But really does it matter
When darkness bleeds both sides?

Waves of Lies

I soak my pages of the Bible in ashes
With grain alcohol
And pin them on the clothesline
To dry in the everlasting
Purifying wind

Waves of lies wash over your mind like the burgeoning tide

I soak my pages of the Bible in ashes
With grain alcohol
And pin them on the clothesline
To dry in the everlasting
Purifying wind

Waves of lies wash over your mind like the burgeoning tide

I soak my pages of the Bible in ashes
With grain alcohol
And pin them on the clothesline
To dry in the everlasting
Purifying wind

Waves of lies wash over your mind like the burgeoning tide

We All Fall Down

Castles fly in the air
Leaves cascade from the sky
World counting time
I don't want to die

I could have had it all
But we all fall down

Cities rise cities perish
Rivers ride the storms to the sea
People are everywhere
But they don't notice me

I could have had it all
But we all fall down

Coffins are all around
Coffins buried in the ground
People don't bury me
I haven't been here too long

We could have had it all
But we all fall down

Discover meaning in the words you say
Today could be your final day
The only memories to play
Are how others saw you make your way

You could have had it all
But we all fall down

We Are All Going Down

Does it hurt?
Yeah it hurts
The pain in flesh or the pain in Heart
You stumble towards the Door
Your blood rages
At your neglect
At your abuse
But who are you to complain?
We are all going down

People try to save us
Mostly they don't care
There are others waiting
It's understandable
You cannot shoulder the weight of Humanity
Or the World

It's because of You
It's because of You
It's because of You
We are all going down

Does it hurt?
Yeah it hurts
The pain in flesh or the pain in Heart
I stumble towards the Door
My blood rages
At my neglect
At my abuse
But who am I to complain?
We are all going down

People try to save us
But mostly we don't care
There are others waiting
It's understandable
We cannot shoulder the weight of Humanity
Or the World

It's because of Me
It's because of Me
It's because of Me
We are all going down

Webby

There's a spider in my hair
And it dances everywhere
Give it food
Give it life
Give it water and air

Step into my mind

Swelling doubt
Vast frustrations
Here we dwell
This situation
This side of Hell
Killing fields
And sweet sensations
Drown them all
In machinations

The other side of the rain

Bought and sold
Hand and soul
The slow maddening into chaos
Holy bound
Crusty clowns
All the way down
Down
Down

Falling into the same old traps are we?

We Need This

Sea salt in the air
River like a mirror
The sink is plugged
And the water is still running

We need this

How do you survive?
You survive because you're still alive
It's nice to feel alive
To be scared and really feel life

We need this

Comfort makes you stall
It makes you disconnect
And not appreciate it all
Yes… we are indeed small

We need this

A lake before my eyes
No more land
Darkened skies
But me?

I feel fine

We need this

When Death is at My Door

Will you come and see me?
When Death is at my door
When Death is at my door
When Death is at my door
Will you come and feel me?
When Death is at my door

Will the Gods appease me?
When Death is at my door
When Death is at my door
When Death is at my door
Will the Gods conceive me?
When Death is at my door

Powerful
Pervading
The dust of Life
This touch of mine
Intoxication
Stains me
This red of wine
This warm delight

When will Love fulfill me?
Before breath is no more
Before breath is no more
Before breath is no more
When will Love bereave me?
Before breath is no more

When the Flames Are Coming Out of the Grill and it is Melting Turn it Off

I'll tell you once
Like I told the others
Don't go rolling with crazy lovers
She screams so loud
You know she fakes it
She'll steal you broke and leave you naked

Here she comes
I see you shaking
Sizzling like some crazy bacon
You bend so hard
Your knees are breaking
She rides you hard like her vacation

Idle vice
A personal sacrifice
I'm not sure what I'm waiting for
But I don't care anymore
I'm just sure that I'm never sure
And the answers are poor

I had a love and it flew away
And in my mind it burns each day
It burns
It burns
It burns

And I don't know what is worse
Dying in darkness
Or the light of the Human curse
I'm drinking more than height or girth
And I know it isn't good

Claim your fight
Nobody is wrong or right
In an Age of Rage
Nobody turns the page
It's always blame
Blame
Blame
Blame

How can anyone give a care?
How can anyone be sane?
How can anyone behave?
Is there gonna be a Civil War?
I've been here before
Way down deep inside Myself
Where I find there is nobody Else

I'm sorry…
Where was I?

Oh yeah
The grill is on fire

When You Were Midnight

Nothing real could shatter glass
When you were Midnight
When you were Midnight

Your brave face was your dark mask
When you were Midnight
When you were Midnight

Torch those eyes to ash
You are Night again
You are Night again
Shade those lips to black
You are Night again
You are Night again
Nothing serves the past
You are Night again
You are Night again
I took your body last
You are Night again
You are Night again

Nothing forward could go back
When you were Midnight
When you were Midnight

Your pale face was your dark mask
When you were Midnight
When you were Midnight

When you were Midnight
When you were Midnight

Why Am I afraid?

I'm in love again
You call me on the phone
To tell me you're alone
When I let you in
You're talking trashy tropes
Dashing all my hopes

Pleasure's all you value
Why am I afraid?
Pleasure's all you follow
Why am I afraid?
Pleasure's all you've got
Why am I afraid?
Such a mess we've made
So why am I afraid?

I have lost my mind
Your laughter's not the same
But maybe I'm to blame
Love is such a crime
Your body's just a tool
To get inside of you

Pleasure's all you value
Why am I afraid?
Pleasure's all you follow
Why am I afraid?
Pleasure's all you've got
Why am I afraid?
Such a mess we've made
So why am I afraid?

I'm in love again
You're reaching for your phone
To tell me you're alone
When I let you in
I'm wishing for a sin
To let me in again

Witches

Witches
All of them
Witches who say to love God
Until your transgressions are exposed
And then they say you'll burn
You'll burn in Hell

Then you pay for it

Mother fucking Witches
And demonic Warlocks
They burn tonight
And they burn bright
And they Goddamn count their money
In the bright white light

Then you pay for it

Sadistic teachings
Boy, they control the World
And you drink your fill
With your hands raised high
And your eyes streaming with tears
As they fuck your children and your soul

Then you pay for it

Death to all
Someone is singing
Death to all
Someone is screaming
Death to all
I have become witness
I must go now

Before I pay for it

Why Bother

Filling in time
Waiting to die
Living a lie
I've got nothing to do
Nothing to prove
Nothing to lose
I can't even move
So paralyzed
I look at the news
And it's DEATH and DISMEMBERMENT
PAIN and CRYING
SPOILEDYOUNGBRATSTHATARESTEALINGANDLYING
Why are we striving?
How are we good?
Consuming food
Plastics and booze
Everything is IN and OUT
But little ABOUT
I ask myself WHY
And the answer is DIE
Because that's the larger part of LIFE

Fried
Frazzled
Bludgeoned
Bedazzled
I've spilled out my guts
I don't know what's what
And all of it doesn't seem to matter
So why bother
Why BOTHER

Whispering Bay Lane

Useless conversations
Down on Whispering Bay Lane
Wind blows through leaves of Eucalyptus

Why did I come here?
Why do I have to go through this?
I have to go back

Could I ever forgive my Father?
For bringing me to this place?
Down on Whispering Bay Lane

It matters doesn't it?
How I leave please tell me
Wind blows through leaves of Eucalyptus

Hold on to that feeling
Things will turn things will not
My Mother isn't home

Naked I walk down Whispering Bay Lane
Wind blows through leaves of Eucalyptus
Never to return

Work It Out

Sneak into the City
Playing with your titties
You're sucking booze
You're blowing cock
You're clamorous and pretty

Gonna dim the lights
Gonna shine tonight
It's all legs and leather
An Ostrich feather
Fishnet sex and sight

Pen and paper
Paint the Town
Write it down
Write it down

Legs and leather
Heel and gown
Write it down
Write it down

Lay down on your backside
Spread your legs and open wide
Now there is moaning
Now there is groaning
Taking it all inside

Pen and paper
Paint the Town
Write it down
Write it down

Legs and leather
Heel and gown
Write it down
Write it down

Lay down on your backside
Work it out
Work it out
Work it out
Work it out

Wisdom

You listen more than you talk
You read more than you watch
You search more than you're sought
You share more than you take
You make more than you've bought
You're real more than you're fake
Unless you are not

Yeah, I'm Trouble

A crazy person walks the street
Noticed by everyone
And by no one

Yeah, I'm trouble

Kill yourself
Call the Police
Kill yourself
Call the Police

Are you crazy?
Of course you are
But crazy is as crazy does

Yeah, I'm trouble

Do operations kill?
Of course they do
As understood

Bombing
Bruising
Lambasting all

Kill yourself
Call the Police
Kill yourself
Call the Police

Yeah, I'm trouble

It resonates
But not for you
For everybody else it's true

Casualty
Is non-compliant
So go your own way unimpeded

Kill yourself
Call the Police
Kill yourself
Call the Police

Yeah, I'm trouble

People die
As they should
But crazy people would

Yeah, I'm trouble

A crazy person
Sitting at his desk
Pushes the button
Pulls the trigger
Lets things go
Signs the papers
Gets things done
But he doesn't walk the streets
He just keeps on going
Making money
Justifying
And he gets things

Yeah, I'm trouble

You Can Ask

Part of me longs for her
A part of me that's lost
Time can induce a fissure in your soul
Reeking with ruminations and regrets
Every stone that was left unturned
And the quiet future you never met

Myriad the dreams and fantasies prevail
Ill to the taste and dull to the touch
Love is not a feeling tossed into the fray
Longing lingers into cold dismay
Empty hearts discarded along the path
You can ask

You Don't See Me

I'm as dumb as a doorknob
I'm as smart as a cookie
I'm a bat in the belfry
I'm as big as a nookie

And you don't see me

I'm as kind as a kitty
I'm as soft as a pillow
I'm as free as a feather
And I weep like a Woman

And you don't see me

I will know to live
I will know to die
Living in my skin
Awkward and lost
And that name is erased from Time

Because you don't see me

You Move

Walls move
They're sharp but they move
With your gun on your back
And your hide saddle pack
You move

Water splashes eyes
Hand swats flies
You move

Clouds move
They're high but they move
You soon burn what you own
Kick the can down the road
You move

Boots stomp grit
Throat clears spit
You move

Time moves
It's short but it moves
You can hum a long song
When your hope is all gone
But you move

I walk the fire
Following you
I move

APPENDIX I

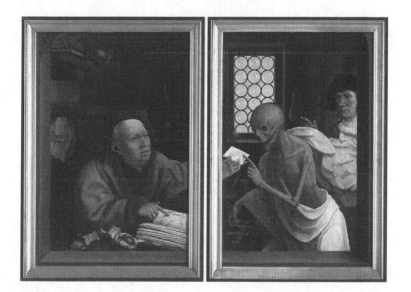

On Becoming a Zombie

There may come a day when you become a Zombie. On that day, there is a pretty good chance that most other people will become Zombies, too.

Becoming a Zombie isn't pretty. In fact, it is a horrible, degrading experience. Think of the worst thing that has ever happened to you. It is infinitely worse than that.

When you first become a Zombie, you will experience dying. That in itself is painful enough. But then it gets worse...

Because you will arise again in a state that is neither living nor dead. Or, to look at it another way, you will be both living *and* dead... at the same time. This will drive you horribly mad.

Your body will rot as in death; a slow, aching rot. And you will feel it, though somewhat numbly. It will be a creepy sensation. You will become abhorrently disgusted with yourself. But because you are insane, you won't know what to do about it.

As a Zombie, you will be a walking figment of your former self. Your blood will cease to flow in your veins and will become clotted black and thick. There will be no thump in your chest because your heart will have ceased functioning. All of your other inner organs will cease functioning as well. You will still be able to walk, maybe even run somewhat, but your muscles and joints will be stiff and it will be painful. But most of your senses will still work to some degree.

You will still be able to see, but your eyesight will be cloudy and it will hurt to move your eyes, and you will be confused by what you see. Objects will seem familiar to you, but you will not be able to work anything, or even remember that things worked in a certain way. This will cause you to become aimless and bumbling. You will be familiar enough with Manmade places to be attracted to them, but you won't know what to do when you get to where they are.

You will hear sounds, but you won't know what they mean. Sudden or loud sounds will draw your attention, but the source will reveal little interest, unless the sounds are generated by living Humans. Your response time to sounds will become greatly inhibited and the confusion behind what they are. Their cause and your abridged response to the will give you a sense of insecurity and will generate much frustration.

As a Zombie, you will still be able to smell, but only marginally, and most of what you smell all the time is the corruption of rot and death that permeates your insides and surroundings. You will not register that what you smell has any meaning, so you will not rely on your smell for navigation or information.

Your mouth will cause you much distress. Your lungs will no longer breathe, but they can still take in air. So, you will rasp in a parody of breathing, even though you don't need to breathe. It will just be an action that you still think you need to do. When you become frustrated or want something you will still make sounds, but they will be grunts and groans and idiot sounds that won't even make sense to you. You will still be able to taste, too, but all you will taste is the putrescence of the filth and decay inside your mouth.

But the sense of taste goes much deeper for a Zombie. You will feel so appalled by the barren emptiness of your body and stomach, so fouled by the cruddy and sour fetidness of your taste that you will crave only two things:

Flesh + Blood

But it goes even deeper than that. Your driving goal will be the end of the state of your Zombification. When you see a living Human you will be so filled with primal jealousy that you will seek to either absorb their life force through the mastication of their flesh and the devouring of their blood, or you will want them to destroy you.

On this, the Zombie will force the issue every time. Living Human flesh will tear easily with your undeniable intentions and it will taste good in your mouth, relieving it of the normally awful taste. And living blood will soothe your parched and ragged throat, filling your stomach with wholesome relief.

But this situation lasts only briefly. For what comes out of a living body dies very quickly and you will feel the aching empty horror of your desecrated body come roaring back. This will cause an overwhelming dismay.

Zombies who exist for any significant length of time soon come to desire not the brief respite of consuming the living, but rather they long to be given what only the living can provide... death. And they will cavort and clamor their way to any weapon, trap, or danger that the living can devise and thrust upon them. For though you will feel an unimaginable desolate torment at being a Zombie, and you will hate yourself and your existence, Zombies are incapable of knowing how to kill themselves, except at the hands of a living Human.

Living creatures, other than Humans, do not attract a Zombie's attention or taste. This is because Zombies have a limited attention span, even more so now that they are Zombies. Think about it. Animals are around us all the time. How many people actively notice all the birds or cows or bugs around them throughout the day? Most of them don't unless they have pets, work on a farm, or work with animals. Most living Humans concentrate on other living Humans.

So it is with Zombies, except even more so. A Zombie, due to their nature and taste, is even more attuned to Human activity and even less aware of other living things. Such is the curse of a Zombie. But it is good for other living things... just not so much for living Humans.

Living Humans are deathly afraid of Zombies, so much so that they will kill them without hesitation and with no regard that the Zombie was once a living person. Zombies make Humans sick, because let's face it: Zombies are disgustingly loathsome. But when Humans are in a relatively safe place, their fear of Zombies can turn to humor.

Humans will mess with Zombies, if they can get away with it. They will take pot shots at them with weapons from rooftops. They will corral them into fortified rings to fight one another. They will cut off Zombie extremities just to see how the Zombie will react and embarrass itself. And all the while they will laugh and joke about it at the Zombie's expense. They'll even use a Zombie's head as a sports ball and kick it around, carefully avoiding the mouth.

Humans know that a Zombie's brain is the only thing keeping it going, and their sense of superiority allows them to exploit the Zombie for personal amusement. This is particularly embarrassing and degrading for the Zombie and it fills them with a great frustration and hatred of living Humans.

There is a certain sense of revenge Humans harbor for Zombies for ruining their world and making existence more complicated than it used to be. The same sense of revenge resides in Zombies, as well, but on a more rudimentary level. This sense of revenge unites both Zombies and living Humans on a common path: either a path of survival, or a path of death. The difference is that living Humans have more options to express themselves regarding the matter... while Zombies are severely limited, other than their sheer numbers.

I don't think anyone knows exactly how long a Zombie can live (or should the term be "persist"), but if you live long enough as a Zombie you will probably regret it. As a Zombie, you will have to contend with the fact that you will eventually just rot away. As your ligaments freeze up and your muscles and skin slough off you will eventually just become a Zombie head, for a brain in a Zombie is the last thing to go, if a living Human or circumstance doesn't get to it first.

At that point, you will just be a rolling, skeletal Zombie head. And there will be no doubt that you will be very disturbed and incensed at your fate. Which is why, if you ever become a Zombie, you should go to where Humans are; there is a good chance that they will kill you off and put you out of your misery. Although you might be inclined to, don't go off somewhere to decompose alone.

There is little honor in being a Zombie and there is even less in dying alone as one.

APPENDIX II

The Dying American

San Bernardino made me want to drink. This relic of culture. Long, flat, and heavily polluted. There was a perpetual twilight to the place. Or maybe it was the ever-present haze, moving in a facsimile of weather and clouds, but laid brown and grey and stale over the city like the culmination of all the failed endeavors of its citizens to parody the act of civilization.

Not a normal person walked its streets; only caricatures of a consumption-based video culture. Only, the consumption was that of destitution and poverty, and the video a pornography of abuse and despair.

The pen I fell into still bore the distinct signature stench of a smoking room turned non-smoking. It leveraged down its saturation upon me as the city leveraged down the despair upon its denizens... a sullen semblance of routine that to them was the way of Life: that something better always belonged to a distant privilege or a different Race.

Out of the window sprawled an empty lot – a flat graveled testament to something that once was: something now demolished. Beyond was a rotted and abandoned mall whose second life was the main backdrop to an apocalyptic Zombie flick, should some prominent B-movie Director come strolling by to receive the inspiration and glory.

Behind the internationally recognized name of the hotel I retired the night to existed the fire gutted skeletal remains of an apartment complex, desperately clinging to the notion that it, too, could be reduced to a vacant lot, perhaps to be built up again anew for some brief respite at mediocrity.

And across the way from my transient abode, Mr. Lee's served up cheap, greasy Chow Mein and cloyingly sweet Orange Chicken from behind barred and gated windows. I bought it, along with tall cans of beer from the local anonymous market... and I choked it down gratefully.

For one pathetic, self-indulgent night I embraced my newfound abnormality: the sick underbelly existence of a Dying American in a Dying Nation. I gazed with paranoid fascination through the door peephole at an empty hall, another bland door staring back at me. I listened furtively to the bumps and clanks resonating from beyond the walls, most of which I presumed to be Human activity, but which could have easily been acts of Beastiality or Cthulhuian summoning rituals.

I parted the gauzy curtains to reveal a neon lit patchwork of vacant tension, periodically broken by the warbling determination of sirens. Occasionally, a dark hooded wraith slumped along the sidewalk with a rhythmic gait.

Why my life should be any different…

For one night, I tasted a despair and defeat both alien and familiar to me. For one night, I consumed it.

ABOUT THE AUTHOR AND THE BOOK

Scott has a BA in Psychology from Sonoma State University. He has always been interested in art, writing, and music and resides in Guerneville, CA, with his 2 Turkish Angora cats: Monkey and Flower.

Photo/Art Credits: No changes were made to the original files, except resizing, and all were sourced from Public Domain.

- Front Cover Photo: **Pluto's Blue Atmosphere in the Infrared** (2016) – NASA

- Back Cover Artwork: **An Old One** (1981) – Tom Ardans' artwork based on H. P. Lovecraft's short novel *At the Mountains of Madness*
- Interior Title Page Artwork: **Saul and the Witch of Endor** (19th Century) – Edward Henry Corbould
- Hierophant Title Page Artwork: **Cthulhu**, portrait (Unknown)
- Introduction Artwork: **Nyarlathotep the Black Pharaoh** (2019) – by Katharsisdrill
- On Becoming a Zombie Artwork: **Death and the Miser** (16th Century) – Jan Provoost
- The Dying American Artwork: **Drunk Father** (1923/1924) – George Bellows
- About the Author and the Book Photo (2019) – **Scott Byorum**

The concepts and ideas expressed in this book are of the author's interpretive imagination only, but based on his real experiences.

Printed in the United States
By Bookmasters